Pharisee
set free

Pharisee
set free

Abandoning religion to seek the heart of God

Emily Fieg

Pharisee Set Free
Copyright © 2020 Emily Fieg

All rights reserved. No part of this publication may be reproduced, stored in or introduced into a retrieval system, or transmitted, in any form, or by any means (electronic, mechanical, photocopying, recording, or otherwise), without the prior permission of the publisher.

Published by Step In Hope LLC
StepInHope.com

ISBN: 978-1-7348609-0-0 (Paperback)
ISBN: 978-1-7348609-1-7 (Ebook)

Library of Congress Control Number: 2020906187

Printed in the United States of America.

Cover Design Copyright © 2020 Emily Fieg
Art Direction by Coty Sloan
www.foxandhounddesign.com
Cover Photo by Sergio Souza on Unsplash

A. NIV - Scripture quotations marked (A) are taken from the Holy Bible, NEW INTERNATIONAL VERSION®, NIV® Copyright © 1973, 1978, 1984, 2011 by Biblica, Inc.® Used by permission. All rights reserved worldwide.

B. ESV - Scripture quotations marked (B) are from the ESV® Bible (The Holy Bible, English Standard Version®), copyright© 2001 by Crossway Bibles, a publishing ministry of Good News Publishers. Used by permission. All rights reserved.

C. NASB - Scripture quotations marked (C) are taken from the New American Standard Bible® (NASB), Copyright © 1960, 1962, 1963, 1968, 1971, 1972, 1973, 1975, 1977, 1995 by The Lockman Foundation. Used by permission. www.Lockman.org

D. NKJV – Scripture quotations marked (D) are taken from the New King James Version. Copyright © 1982 by Thomas Nelson, Inc. Used by permission. All rights reserved.

E. NLT - Scripture quotations marked (E) are taken from the Holy Bible, New Living Translation, copyright ©1996, 2004, 2015 by Tyndale House Foundation. Used by permission of Tyndale House Publishers, a Division of Tyndale House Ministries, Carol Stream, Illinois 60188. All rights reserved.

F. MSG – Scripture quotations marked (F) are taken from The Message. Copyright Â© 1993, 1994, 1995, 1996, 2000, 2001, 2002. Used by permission of NavPress Publishing Group.

G. AMP - Scripture quotations marked (G) are taken from the Amplified® Bible (AMP), Copyright © 2015 by The Lockman Foundation. Used by permission. www.Lockman.org

H. GNT - Scriptures marked as (H) are taken from the Good News Translation - Second Edition © 1992 by American Bible Society. Used by permission.

I. TPT - Scripture quotations marked (I) are from The Passion Translation®. Copyright © 2017, 2018 by Passion & Fire Ministries, Inc. Used by permission. All rights reserved. ThePassionTranslation.com.

Dedication

To my precious children - You are a bit too little to read this yet, but I press in harder on my own journey for your sake. I know I will fail you at times, but I trust that God will redeem even my mistakes for your good. May you always know the depth of God's love for you and have faith to move mountains. God has amazing plans for you!

Contents

Preface	1
Introduction	3
Chapter 1 - The Church	11
Chapter 2 - Pharisees	27
Chapter 3 - Theology Versus Faith	37
Chapter 4 - Encountering God	55
Chapter 5 - Incomplete Understanding	67
Chapter 6 - Tactics of the Enemy	79
Chapter 7 - Our Identity	97
Chapter 8 - The Holy Spirit	109
Chapter 9 - The Acts of the Holy Spirit	121
Chapter 10 - God's Miraculous Power	131
Chapter 11 - Hearing God's Voice	153
Chapter 12 - Our Testimony	165
Acknowledgements	169
Resources	173
About the Author	174

Preface

God began putting this book on my heart in a very informal way in January 2019. At that time, all I had was an idea from Him: My Nicodemus Story. I honestly wasn't too serious about it. It was just a passing thought that I wrote down.

Then, on a Wednesday in September 2019, God grabbed my attention and told me it was time to write the book. Not only that, but He told me to write it in 30 days, and He told me clearly that it was supposed to include my personal story of becoming so much more than a born-again Pharisee.

I wasn't totally sold. I was not sure about the timeline. I put it off for a few days. Maybe longer. But then God told me again and reaffirmed what I was called to do. So here I am, 30 days from that Wednesday in September, finishing my rough draft and writing a preface.

The book has ended up being my personal story combined with quite a bit of in-depth study of Scripture, and questions for you to consider which might take you deeper into your own walk with the Lord. It is intended to be uplifting while providing a safe place for you to examine what you believe and why, while I share my own experiences along the way.

I am still a bit hesitant. I don't particularly like sharing important parts of who I am with people I don't know and fully trust. I like to protect myself. Writing a book sharing many of my deepest personal experiences and sharing my heart was not on my list of things I wanted to do. I thought I might write a book one day—fiction maybe, since it's my favorite, or something impersonal. But God called me to write this book—with my story—at this time.

This book is my testimony, but it is also more than that. I offer you, the reader, an opportunity to look at your own faith and theology and answer questions that perhaps no one has ever asked you. It's also about the church today and how it can hinder people, about stepping into the new identity you have in Christ, and about really getting to know God—not just who you think He is. He's been misrepresented by so many people.

There is no way to fully and correctly represent God—so forgive me where I fail to do Him justice. He is so much more than could ever fit into a book, and He's already got a really good one (or 66) written by Him.

Hopefully you will come out of this with a stronger, deeper faith, whether you agree or disagree with where I've ended up. More than anything, my goal is for you to find more of the abundant life, hope, and joy that you've been promised in the Scriptures, and that you would see what is possible and available to you as a child of God.

There have been many people in my life who were part of my faith journey over the years. This is not a book to condemn anyone. The fact that I am here is a testament to the influence of many godly people in my life. Each part of my journey was important in order for me to arrive where I am now.

I am incredibly thankful for all I learned along the way, my grounding and knowledge of Scripture, and the friendships and guidance from other believers. I wish I had understood some of the truths in this book sooner, but somehow God's timing is always perfect, even if we feel we are running late. So, let's dive in. I hope you'll be challenged and encouraged by what you read.

Introduction

By the grace God has given me, I laid a foundation as a wise builder, and someone else is building on it. But each one should build with care. For no one can lay any foundation other than the one already laid, which is Jesus Christ. If anyone builds on this foundation using gold, silver, costly stones, wood, hay or straw, their work will be shown for what it is, because the Day will bring it to light. It will be revealed with fire, and the fire will test the quality of each person's work. If what has been built survives, the builder will receive a reward. If it is burned up, the builder will suffer loss but yet will be saved—even though only as one escaping through the flames.

- 1 Corinthians 3:10-15 [A]

No one sets out to be a Pharisee, it just happens little by little over the years. If you've spent any time reading the gospels, you know the Pharisees and Sadducees are the bad guys. Little kids in Sunday school even know this. Jesus is good. Pharisees are bad. So, discovering I was a Pharisee turned my world upside-down. You see, I thought I was safe from being a Pharisee because I am "born again" and have been for many years.

A couple of years ago, sharing my testimony would have meant sharing mostly details from my younger years, starting with how I accepted Jesus at a young age, all the growing and struggles and recommitments I made as I went through my school years, and my early years of marriage. Those years, experiences, and growth were important. It was in those years I learned to love the Bible. I memorized Scripture, studied it, and dug deep.

Pharisee Set Free

I discovered the value of tithing. I studied biblical principles of marriage which have greatly blessed my relationship with my husband. I learned to talk to God, to wrestle with God, and to come out stronger. I examined and considered church doctrine and theology. I am so thankful for many of the foundational things I learned in those years.

But my testimony that needs to be shared now is one that only starts about two years ago. By that point in my life, I felt solid in my faith. I'd been attending church, reading my Bible, praying faithfully, and having a quiet time for years. I regularly attended and even led Bible studies. I was doing pretty good at what I felt my purpose as a Christian was—I followed the rules, lived a moral life, and had faith in God, even when bad things happened because I trusted that God was working out something in my life.

Occasionally, a scary thought would cross my mind as I read certain passages in the Bible—the thought that I looked a lot like a Pharisee with all my rules and religious acts and accomplishments. But I would encourage myself that I was superior and "safe" because I believed in Jesus and because of my "born again" status.

I imagine you're saying that counts for something—and it does. It is critically important. But, if Jesus came in the flesh and saw the church today, what would He say to the Christian sects of our day? We have an idea from what He said to the Pharisees. We will look at those scriptures in the chapters ahead. And I would submit that there is a new type of Pharisee He would address—a "born again" Pharisee. I was one of those "born again" Pharisees.

We also have more insight on what Jesus might say by looking at what He said to the churches in the book of Revelation. In Revelation 2:4[B] God says, "But I have this against you, that you have abandoned the love you had at first." Then in Revelation 3:15[C] He says, "I know your deeds, that you are neither cold nor hot; I wish that you were cold or hot." I'd say that described me. I knew it shouldn't, but I couldn't figure out how to be what I should.

I had a lot in common with the Pharisees of Jesus' time but not a lot in common with Jesus or with the disciples after the Holy Spirit came upon them. 2 Timothy 3:5 talks about avoiding people who have a form of godliness but deny its power, and I was one of those people. I was always worried that I was a branch about to be cut off (John 15:2), but I didn't know how to be a branch that produced fruit.

Sure, I did godly things: I read the Bible and prayed and went to church regularly. I served in the church and led Bible studies and tithed faithfully. But I wondered inside if that was really the main fruit I was supposed to bear. And since the Holy Spirit lived within me, why didn't I see more progress, more fruit, and why didn't I look like the disciples in the book of Acts?

I had so much head knowledge, knew so much doctrine and theology, but all of that was doing very little for my heart. I liked to pretend it was heart knowledge, because I knew that was important, and I did have *some* heart knowledge. I had heard God speak to my heart. My desire was to know and follow His will for my life. I'd had special moments with God. But looking back on it, the heart knowledge I had was just a few drops in the bucket compared to what it could have been.

1 Corinthians 8:1b-3^c says, "we know that we all have knowledge. Knowledge makes arrogant, but love edifies. If anyone supposes that he knows anything, he has not yet known as he ought to know; but if anyone loves God, he is known by Him."

My status as a Pharisee wasn't because I didn't have Jesus in my heart. It was because I had my core beliefs out of order. I thought knowledge of the Bible, being right, and not having any holes in my logic or theology was crucial to a strong faith. I believed God cared most about morality. I was taught that sin was the enemy. I thought trying hard was all I could do. I was proud of how much I knew and the things that I did, but I was also condemned and shamed by anything I did wrong.

I, like the Pharisees, was more concerned about setting up extra rules and boundaries so I and the people I was responsible for, especially my children, wouldn't fall prey to sin. I had made morality equally as important as believing in Jesus.

For example, I set up rules about the types of music, books, and videos I or my kids could enjoy. And I set up boundaries about the clothing we wore and the activities we did. But the boundaries actually hurt more than they helped, because they were against sin rather than toward relationship with God. The boundaries brought resistance and caused disagreements. And when we really wanted to, we could find loopholes.

When I created boundaries out of a need to keep the law, they didn't engage our hearts. Now I have new boundaries, but they are born out of love for the Lord, not out of rule following and fear. My love for the Lord now forms boundaries that I'm not tempted to break.

Don't misunderstand me: Knowing the truth is key, being obedient to God's moral laws is important, and sin is bad. Nonetheless, something more important must first be built on the solid foundation.

My family and I enjoy going to rocky beaches in Washington state and gathering rocks to stack. We all make our own tower of rocks, often competing to see whose stack has the most rocks. The thing about building rock stacks is that you can stack the rocks in any order as long as they don't fall.

If you have several similar-sized stones, you may have to work to figure out the best order to place them in. Sometimes a smaller flat or square rock can go under a larger or wider rock if it provides a firm building

Introduction

surface. Sometimes you use other small rocks to add support under an unsteady one. I've seen people stack rocks in the most unbelievable ways, finding the natural balance points and working for hours to place them just right.

In many ways, our faith is like a rock stack. We all know the foundation and cornerstone rock at the bottom is Jesus. But as the verse at the beginning of this chapter says, we all, individually, build on that foundation. In the Scriptures, we've been given a pile of truths that we are trying to balance on the foundation. But sometimes, because of the order we put them in, we must add other little rocks, that are not part of the truths, to support them. Sometimes we just stack them in an unsteady order. Unlike the physical rocks, we don't always know the shape and weight and balance of each truth.

I would submit this is why Christians often come to places of crisis. When your stack is unbalanced or propped up by outside ideas that are not core truths, and life or the enemy brings winds of pain or misfortune or loss, your rocks can begin to fall.

I had learned all the biblical truths my teachers and parents wanted to teach me. I'd just learned to stack them in the wrong order. I'd also added a lot of other small rocks that were not core truths. They were either other theologies I'd been taught, or they were my own reasoning that I used to support certain core truths. I needed them to prop up parts of my faith tower that seemed unstable. I'd always felt somewhat uncomfortable with some of those small rocks, and even some large ones, because while I knew Scriptures that seemed to confirm them, I also knew Scriptures that seemed to contradict them.

The enemy likes to help us solidify distortions in the stack and turn it into a religious rock stack by having us add some glue of pride and self-righteousness to make sure nothing budges. My old stack was unbalanced, but you wouldn't know it because I'd glued the unbalanced rocks in place with pride. As you look at your faith stack, look for those areas where pride has snuck in. Pride is the mark of the enemy and the reason for his fall from Heaven.

I had come to believe that I needed a theology that explained everything. I learned from highly educated people about many possible holes in my faith stack and in the Bible and then agreed with them on how to patch them up. Additionally, I wanted my theology to explain my own and other people's experiences in a way that made sense.

Many people have tried to explain why bad things happen, but in my desire for a theology that did so, I ended up distorting who God is into something He's not. I exchanged what love means, what good means, what kindness means for something that looked similar but wasn't at all the same. I did all this because I needed my faith stack to explain a god who let church leaders hurt the people they were over, who gave people cancer to grow them in their faith, and who caused people to die in order to bring others to salvation.

I had not yet come to understand that just because God helps someone grow in their faith as a result of having cancer doesn't mean He gave them cancer. I knew Romans 8:28[D], "And we know that all things work together for good to those who love God, to those who are the called according to His purpose." But I hadn't learned that He can be the author of the good without being the author of the bad.

My understanding was that since God was sovereign, then He was actively controlling everything. And if He was actively in control of everything, then He must be behind all the bad things. This thinking led to helplessness. It led to futile thinking. It led to fear of when God was going to give me something bad to then turn into good. On top of that, I was so caught up in the moral and academic, so focused on not leaving any room for failure, that I missed the heart of God. I was ignoring the basic truth that He loves us so very much.

Introduction

We will look more deeply at these concepts in the chapters ahead. But before we do, I invite you to take a minute to consider these questions:

1. What core theologies are the basis of your belief system? What theologies in your belief stack do you suspect may be out of order?

2. What areas of your Christian life are you proud of? Are any of them areas where you are relying on self-effort and works? Which of these areas could potentially be out of alignment with God and Scripture?

3. Do you have any Bible verses that are catching points for you? Ones that you read, and you believe, but a small part of you wonders if you've missed something? What examples come to mind?

4. In what areas of your life do you fear failure? What protective and safe boundaries have you set up so you can't fail? How do you do this in your Christian faith?

5. Which beliefs or thought patterns described most resonate with you?

CHAPTER 1

The Church

Whoever has ears, let them hear what the Spirit says to the churches. To the one who is victorious, I will give the right to eat from the tree of life, which is in the paradise of God.

- Revelation 2:7[A]

The idea of church often evokes a powerful emotion from people. Those on the outside may not know much about Jesus but, at least in first world countries, they know about the church and often have strong opinions of it. Today, people are leaving the church at an alarming rate, and well-known Christians are leaving in very public ways.

Some leave due to the abuses they see in the church. Others leave because the church is not bringing transformation and life and all that Jesus promised. They wanted more but have not been shown how to receive what is available, and now believe there is nothing more. Many people actually view the secular world as more loving and fruitful than believers.

For most of my life, the church has been a good place for me. Many times, being at church even felt like being home. I have had many wonderful Christian mentors over the years. I don't know if I would have considered them mentors at the time, but looking back I can name many from different churches and seasons in my life who had an impact on my journey. My family is also full of believers and godly examples who have taught and encouraged me.

Over the years, though, I have also had a few powerfully negative experiences with Christians and the church. This is not the place to list them, but I know I am not alone. I have met so many people who have been hurt by the church. People fail—Christians and church leaders included—and most of us have wounds from those we looked up to most. And we may have even failed others in our role as Christians or leaders, although that was obviously not our intent.

When we view Christians and church leaders as God's representatives, and then they fail us or harm us or teach us incorrectly, we end up with a distorted view of who God is. The church is supposed to reflect the heart of God, but many times it does almost the opposite. Does the world see the church as a loving and safe place? To sinners, Jesus was loving and compassionate. Only to the hypocritical religious sects and their leaders was He harsh and critical.

God cares how church leaders treat the church body. Paul and Peter both spent time telling the church the requirements for godly leaders. In 1 Peter 5:2-3[B], Peter says, "shepherd the flock of God that is among you, exercising oversight, not under compulsion, but willingly, as God would have you; not for shameful gain, but eagerly; not domineering over those in your charge, but being examples to the flock."

It breaks God's heart when we have been hurt in the church. Our negative experiences there can lead us to believe false things about Him. God wants to show us where we have developed a distorted view of Him and show us instead who He really is. Sometimes the distortion is so far into the foundation of our faith that God must do major reconstruction to fix the foundation.

A couple of years ago, my husband and I found ourselves needing a change. We had some spiritual wounds that were not going to heal in the church where we were. We were desperate for something transformative. We also had some major challenges that we seemed to be battling without support, especially trying to find loving and effective ways to parent our young children. We often felt alone, frustrated, and exhausted.

In my mind, I had all these possible reasons why I felt that way. I was probably just burned out. Perhaps I needed encouragement. Maybe I wasn't trying hard enough. Could it be that I was making poor choices and being punished? Possibly God was unhappy with me. Perhaps I'd grieved the Holy Spirit. Or maybe I'd quenched the Holy Spirit by ignoring the feeling I needed to do something and not doing it.

I also had questions under the surface that I kept pushing down. Where was the power that I should have to be able to walk out this Christian life? Why did I feel timid? Why was life so hard? Where was the peace that passes understanding? Where was the fruit? Was God about to cut me off the tree like a branch that wasn't producing fruit?

I was in a season where I didn't really like reading the New Testament. Part of me felt I already knew all about Jesus. And the Old Testament people were so much more relatable. They were so flawed and yet God chose and loved them.

I had a hard time relating to a Holy Spirit-filled Peter, Paul, John, or Stephen. Supernatural events didn't show up in my life. The apostles had healed people, spoken boldly, endured hardship with great joy. That wasn't me. I often wondered if I was like the churches in the book of Revelation I mentioned earlier—neither hot nor cold, and about to be spit out. I was lukewarm. But, in the churches and circles I was in, it wasn't normal for people to always be on fire for God.

At that time, our hearts were really being separated from the church we were members of. We began to feel the desire to leave for many reasons, and yet God told us to stay. Or, more specifically, to wait. God started by heavily pressing the importance of unity of the church on my heart. Over and over in different settings, unity of believers showed up everywhere.

So, we tried very hard to find unity and overcome hurts and live in love where we were. And that was such an important thing for us to learn—how to be unified in places of hurt and tension.

We were still serving in a leadership role that we felt was needed—even though we felt ineffective. The teaching at the church was still biblical. We stayed almost two years past our very first thoughts of leaving. And then, suddenly, we felt God tell us it was time to go. Though I'd been waiting for it, my husband still had to encourage me that first week to go someplace new. That first step into the unknown felt risky.

At this point we knew where we were leaving, but not where we were going. The first church we visited was a Baptist church. We enjoyed it a great deal. My husband thought it might be the place. He said we should go back the next week. But I thought we needed to look at more, to be sure.

As we prayed over the next few months, we both separately felt God leading us to look for a more Spirit-filled church. There was no audible voice, just a consistent theme. I kept finding God speaking to me about it in my Bible reading, in random videos, and even in the Beth Moore Bible study I was still attending at my old church.

One day, in the car with my husband, God clearly spoke to me in my mind. He said He would bless us no matter which church we picked from our list, but if we were willing to go out of our comfort zone, He wanted to teach us something new about Himself. These kinds of moments of hearing God so powerfully were very rare in my life. In that moment, I felt God confirming that He was leading us to a more Spirit-led church.

Along the way, we visited all kinds and denominations of churches. We liked a lot of them and felt that biblical teaching was happening at many of them, but just didn't feel God confirming that they were right for us. This process taught us a lot. Firstly, to celebrate and pray for the churches around us because they were bringing truth to our community, even if we didn't end up there. Secondly, about process. Sometimes you need to go through a process to be ready for what God has for you.

We needed to really be convinced that God was calling us to a church that was different from where we were—one where we would learn something new about God. While we were on our journey, God was also preparing the church He was leading us to. We ended up at a relatively new church plant. For us to not overlook it, the church needed to be advanced enough in its growth for us to recognize it as the place God had for us.

By the time we came to the church we now call home, we had been searching for almost four months. In their service that first Sunday, all I could think was that I was experiencing a small taste of what heaven would be like.

The worship was so powerful, and God's presence showed up in a way I had not often experienced. I didn't expect my husband to like it since he's reserved during worship and no one there was being reserved. I decided that even if it was the only time we came, I was going to enjoy being there. What a wonderful blessing when I found out my husband liked the church despite the expressive worshipers!

Honestly, I didn't understand a lot of things that happened in the service that day and in future days. Was the person who led the prayer time speaking in tongues? Why was the congregation making declarations about their own finances before the offering? Did they really think God wanted to heal every single sickness? What were these "words" that people kept getting and giving?

Even though we were unsure about all those things, my husband and I both felt very strongly after our second visit that this was the church God was calling us to. The people were so genuine and welcoming, we already felt like it was home, and we both had a major sense of peace.

We recognized that God's presence showed up powerfully there. We knew we would have a lot of questions, but we also knew God wanted to teach us something new.

I was very adamant about guarding my mind from deception, though. So much of what we experienced there was very different from where I came from. I didn't want to blindly accept everything this church was doing without testing it.

But the other main thing that drew us to the church was that the preaching and teaching was very biblical. The pastor often stopped and explained why they did things like pray in tongues or say the declaration about finances with Scripture. He was also always receptive to questions later. We felt like it was a safe place to learn about some things that were different and to decide what to do if our theology disagreed with those things later.

As I was trying to discern false teachings and prophets, I turned to Scripture to see what it said. I found Matthew 7:15-20[A],

> *Watch out for false prophets. They come to you in sheep's clothing, but inwardly they are ferocious wolves. By their fruit you will recognize them. Do people pick grapes from thornbushes, or figs from thistles? Likewise, every good tree bears good fruit, but a bad tree bears bad fruit. A good tree cannot bear bad fruit, and a bad tree cannot bear good fruit. Every tree that does not bear good fruit is cut down and thrown into the fire. Thus, by their fruit you will recognize them.*

I've realized that Christians are quick to label people they disagree with as false prophets and false teachers without looking at the fruit they produce. I've read criticism of leaders in many different denominations where they've been labelled false teachers or false prophets. Those same leaders being criticized see a lot of good fruit from their ministries.

Ironically, Luke 6:26[A] says, "Woe to you when everyone speaks well of you, for that is how their ancestors treated the false prophets."

I started to look for fruit at this church. I saw people who were open and honest about struggles, but who clearly loved Jesus. These people were passionate about worshiping God. They often had joy in trials. They had faith beyond what I had ever seen. Even more, they loved people well, and were some of the kindest people we'd met. We even saw a few people healed. Their fruit was obvious.

They didn't approve of sin but did value grace. They also didn't pressure me at all into believing as they did. They welcomed questions, told me what they believed, and didn't engage in futile debates, but would respectfully discuss different viewpoints. They were genuine in hoping we would find hope in what they told us, but not in a way that felt weird if we weren't willing to accept what they said.

As I searched the Bible, I also found 2 Peter 2:1-3[A],

> *But there were also false prophets among the people, just as there will be false teachers among you. They will secretly introduce destructive heresies, even denying the sovereign Lord who bought them—bringing swift destruction on themselves. Many will follow their depraved conduct and will bring the way of truth into disrepute. In their greed these teachers will exploit you with fabricated stories. Their condemnation has long been hanging over them, and their destruction has not been sleeping.*

This was harder to judge. How did I know if there were secret destructive heresies if they were secret? They didn't seem to deny the sovereign Lord, but my understanding of how God's sovereignty acted was a little different than theirs. But I could clearly see that they were not doing anything out of greed. They had sacrificed much to be leading this little church that was still finding its footing financially. Even with the "odd" things that happened on Sunday, they were not bringing disrepute to the truth, but rather bringing life and healing to people as a result of believing what they read in the Bible.

Further in 2 Peter 2:18-19[B], it continues teaching about false teachers, saying,

> *For, speaking loud boasts of folly, they entice by sensual passions of the flesh those who are barely escaping from those who live in error. They promise them freedom, but they themselves are slaves of corruption. For whatever overcomes a person, to that he is enslaved.*

In contrast, the people at this church had humility, vulnerability, and didn't try to appeal to the flesh, but always to the Spirit. They did promise freedom, but only because they themselves were experiencing it. They pointed to God the Father, Son, and Holy Spirit to learn how to walk in the freedom Jesus paid for.

Also, I was finally understanding Scriptures I'd been familiar with for a long time. My eyes were being opened to the actual meaning of Scriptures about God's power, about God's kingdom, and about my identity in Christ that I had studied and known and believed in a general way, but now understood in a way that brought clarity and life.

For so long my focus was mostly on sin and morality. That could be because I am naturally inclined to be a rule follower. I want to be a good rule follower, and I want others to follow the rules as well. It is also possible that I am that way because of my Christian upbringing.

The church really likes to talk about sin. They really like to dislike sin and call people out of sin and emphasize overcoming sin, and yet many of the people in church are still slaves to sin. They are not yet walking in their new identity that results from God's victory over sin. We were sinners. Our faith in Christ and His death and resurrection changes our identity.

The Church

Romans 6:6-7^E says, "We know that our old sinful selves were crucified with Christ so that sin might lose its power in our lives. We are no longer slaves to sin. For when we died with Christ we were set free from the power of sin." If you are still overcome by sin, you are not walking in what Jesus paid for on the cross.

The presence of God changed me. The voice of God changed me. The heart of God changed me. Am I perfect? No. But, is my identity still a sinner? No. I am not just a sinner saved by grace. I am a daughter of the King, who walks with God, is filled with the Holy Spirit, and who is called to bring God's will to earth. Do I always succeed? No. Does that change my identity back to a sinner? No. I keep my eyes on Jesus, the author and perfecter of my faith, not the sin that I sometimes step into.

In my old mindset, I never understood David. Why is he called a man after God's heart? He's so emotional. He publicly sinned—breaking quite a few of the ten commandments. He was sometimes impulsive. I didn't think that any church I knew would want David to be in their pulpit.

In addition to his sins, he might end up dancing down the aisle naked, giving passionate and emotional speeches, vacillating between highs and lows in every sermon, getting worked up over something without warning. Not to mention that he hung out with the prophets and killed animals with his bare hands (even if it was to protect the sheep). No church I knew was looking to hire a pastor like that.

So, what kind of pastor did it seem that churches wanted? Some wanted a Saul (the pre-conversion version of Paul)—well educated, rule follower, impeccable background, extremely knowledgeable of the Scriptures. A man passionately against the enemies of the church, determined not to let any heresy in.

Some wanted a mild Paul—the guy who weeps for those in trouble, is passionate, but in a dignified way, willing to preach even to the point of chains—though let's not do anything too risky. They didn't want the more extreme Paul who sent out handkerchiefs he'd touched to heal the sick who received them. (Acts 19:12).

Some wanted what the Jews expected Jesus to be—a person passionate about overthrowing the current political system so that we can live victoriously in a religiously perfect society where God destroys our enemies.

I didn't know of many who wanted a pastor that was truly like Jesus—a pastor who goes and hangs out with the extortionists, the debt collectors, and the prostitutes. They didn't want a pastor who starts his lessons with a healing service and then, when he gets to the message, only speaks in stories and riddles and doesn't give any practical life application to clarify.

No church I knew really wanted a pastor who calls out the hypocrisy within its walls or points out that it isn't bringing life or hope to desperate people. They seemed to want a pastor who placed higher value on those inside the church who follow the rules than those who are sinners on the fringe that are sick and hurting and outcast.

Many churches are looking to soften the gospel to bring people in, but Jesus didn't water down his message to make people more comfortable. Matthew 5:48[C] says, "Therefore you are to be perfect, as your heavenly Father is perfect."

And then the next verse in Matthew 6:1[A] says, "Be careful not to practice your righteousness in front of others to be seen by them. If you do, you will have no reward from your Father in heaven." Jesus' standard would upset those on both the law and the grace sides, the deeply religious and those who want God with no rules.

Jesus loved people and had compassion. He touched the sinners, the diseased, the unclean and sought them out. In the church today, we can miss God's heart for people because we are so concerned about the more

The Church

trivial church "details" such as what type of songs we sing, what type of flooring goes in, what type of small groups the church offers, etc.

Does the pastor preach in a style I like? Does the church only sing songs by Christian artists that have the same theology as mine? Does the church do baptism and communion exactly the way I believe is correct? Do other people in the church think the same way I do?

On the other hand, while the church should try to be respectful of the hearts of its people, the church was not created to cater to and serve the members' every whim. Rather, the church should be us, as the body, building up our brothers and sisters and serving and glorifying God. There is benefit to diversity in the body of Christ and finding unity in our diversity. (1 Corinthians 12)

Another area that can cause disagreement in churches is the Bible translation used. Every church I have attended has had a favorite translation of the Bible. Some prefer the more readable versions in order to reach the unchurched. Some prefer a more accurate word-for-word translation for the sake of being correct and academic. Some prefer a more accurate sentence-by-sentence translation for a closer picture of how it reads in the original text.

Most churches also have translations they judge as inferior. If they care about readability, then the more archaic versions are looked at as less relevant. If they care about accuracy, then modern language Bibles that paraphrase are scorned. Since I have been more concerned about the academic study of the Bible for years, I preferred more direct translations, often comparing two or three of the more academic translations and almost scorning translations like *The Message*.

The Lord has recently been showing me just how profoundly He can speak through *The Message* version. It's not my first choice for study, but for a fresh look at passages I've overanalyzed, it has proven refreshing and draws me deeper into my relationship with Him. Sometimes we need to step back and look with new eyes when we find ourselves stuck in head knowledge.

Different translations have different purposes. I'd heard people talk about the Bible as a love letter. When reading it from an academic standpoint, it was so hard for me to see that. By reading it in a different translation, one I'm less familiar with, I often come away with a fresh understanding. This has allowed me to see God's love poured out for us through the pages.

I've purposely included verses from a number of different translations in this book. Instead of noting the translation in the text, I've included a letter by each direct reference that corresponds to the translation as noted on the copyright page. Feel free to also look up each verse in your favorite translation. But maybe consider if God might want to speak to you through a translation that isn't your first choice.

Now, just as I've stepped back and reexamined the values of different Bible translations, I invite you to take a similar step back with all the non-essential issues we have in the church. Ask yourself:

- Could God be moving in a different but powerful way in an alternate style of worship?
- Could God speak to you in a different type of church small group than you were looking for?
- Is He calling you to start the group you wish your church offered?
- Could God reach the same or different people with a different color carpet or by changing the time church services start?
- Is God saving people through worship music written by an artist whose theology is slightly different from yours?

I am coming to realize that most denominations really do well capturing a certain aspect of God that other denominations may overlook. But some of them have introduced heresies along the way, perhaps because they have overemphasized one aspect of God and thereby deemphasized or changed another aspect of God. By staying in only one denomination, or even in just one non-denominational church, we can really develop a one-dimensional view of God.

I've always looked down on "church hopping" and "church shopping" as if there was some value of being a member at a church the longest, or as if leaving is betraying the church. On the other side, people leave churches for rather petty reasons. Jesus' focus at the end of His life was praying for unity of the believers and the church, so we should also place a high value on it. Unity doesn't necessarily mean agreeing but rather disagreeing in loving ways and honoring each other.

I hope you have a church you really love. I am not advocating leaving that church. If you'd like to see if there are sides of God you might be missing, perhaps start listening to sermons from another denomination a couple times a month. Don't adjust your theology unless you really see more biblical truth, but also don't be so closed off that you miss what God might be saying.

There was something special about visiting a different denomination each week as we looked for a church. God was speaking through His Word in each of them. People were worshiping God at all of them. Were any of them perfect? No. Are any of us perfect? No.

Each church will hopefully have some amazing strengths, possibly unique to themselves, but each will also likely have a few weaknesses. Let's be people who go to church and, instead of criticizing what isn't right, celebrate what is good, and become part of the solution to making it better—with loving others well as our main goal.

Plenty of churches and all denominations have had bad apples. Some televangelists have a poor reputation based on some pretty major problems. I used to judge "Spirit-led" churches based on what I'd heard about them. My theology was different than what they taught. I still see the harm that "Spirit-led" churches can do if their teaching isn't biblical.

Any church and denomination can do great harm to Christians and non-Christians based on what they teach, how they teach it, and the example they show. But there are also plenty of churches in every denomination furthering the gospel, preaching the good news, and being the hands and feet of Jesus. You don't have to have perfect theology to know Jesus, be saved, and be furthering His kingdom on earth.

I can't imagine that any church has everything perfectly understood and emphasized in perfect balance. God and His ways are so far beyond full human comprehension. There are so many aspects of God and so many ways God reveals Himself that we're more than likely going to have some things incorrect. How could a finite mind understand an infinite God?

We also have an adversary who would love for us to build our faith rock stack with half-truths that fit our experience rather than with whole truths found in Scripture. And if we do that, we will continue to need to add more small half-truth stones to support and balance our faith stack. Over time we could end up looking like spiritual Leaning Towers of Pisa. We need to be watchful and analyze areas where we may have begun to be deceived.

But God can be working in any church, even one where leaders have poor motives or values. Paul says in Philippians 1:15-18[A],

> *It is true that some preach Christ out of envy and rivalry, but others out of goodwill. The latter do so out of love, knowing that I am put here for the defense of the gospel. The former preach Christ out of selfish ambition, not sincerely, supposing that they can stir up trouble for me while I am in chains. But what does it matter? The important thing is that in every way, whether from false motives or true, Christ is preached. And because of this I rejoice.*

The Church

Even so, I hope you are not in a church with leaders who hurt the flock. I hope you feel the love of God being poured out at your church. I hope you find a place like I did—a place full of life, love, hope, and passion for God, where you can grow deeper in the Lord in ways you never imagined.

One of the areas I really think our church has a strength is in its willingness to risk possibly looking foolish and possibly even failing in exchange for seeing God show up in miraculous and supernatural ways—ways that draw people to Him and change the world around us for the better. What once made me uncomfortable, I now actively seek out. I now like being part of a church that doesn't set itself up for success whether or not God shows up.

I want to be in a church that is so vulnerable that if God doesn't show up, it's clear—a church that is reaching so far that it will fail, be honest about failing, and try again. I've had the absolute privilege to be able to step out and take risks in a relatively safe environment. How will we be changed if we never see God move? And how will we see God move if we never put ourselves in a place where we need God to move?

I don't have all the answers. I only know that I was a Pharisee who wanted to love God and do good works and make sure everyone was following the law. Now, I see that I'm a daughter who has a place at the Father's table, who is loved no matter what, and who wants to do good works because she likes to feel the joy of her Father.

Before, I saw some fruits of the Spirit, but more fruits of the flesh—fear, frustration, self-focus, despair. Now, God is transforming me—I am filled with more love, joy, peace, generosity, and compassion. I see an increase in all the fruits of the Spirit.

We will look at these topics more in depth later in the book, but for now, consider your own faith. By taking a little time to answer these questions, you can really begin to examine your own heart.

1. Have you ever been at a crossroads in your faith? What happened?

2. What church denomination are you most comfortable with? Why?

3. Which church denomination are you least comfortable with? Why?

4. When is the last time you heard someone say something that was biblically accurate, but in a way that was not in line with the heart of God? How did it affect you?

5. What is your preferred Bible translation? Which translation(s) do you dislike? Do you believe God is able to speak to people through a translation you are uncomfortable with?

6. How often do you feel God's love coming off the pages of the Bible? Do you agree or disagree that the Bible is a love letter to God's people?

7. Do you approach God like a child or like a scholar? Which way do you think is better? Do both have value?

8. How different would your church look on a Sunday morning if God didn't show up? How long would it take for anyone to notice?

9. When was the last time you saw God move in a way that powerfully changed you? Do you allow yourself to be in situations where you need God to show up?

CHAPTER 2

Pharisees

> *And he said to them, "Well did Isaiah prophesy of you hypocrites, as it is written, 'This people honors me with their lips, but their heart is far from me; in vain do they worship me, teaching as doctrines the commandments of men.' You leave the commandment of God and hold to the tradition of men." And he said to them, "You have a fine way of rejecting the commandment of God in order to establish your tradition!"*
>
> - Mark 7:6-9[B]

Scripture is such an integral part of my life. I love searching it and finding new aspects and facets of God. I enjoy seeking further understanding of complex biblical ideas. But merely studying the Scriptures isn't enough.

A person could write countless books, preach a lifetime's worth of sermons, give all their money and time to the church, or compose chart-topping worship songs, all based on their study of Scriptures, without ever actually connecting to the heart of God. How many Christian pastors and authors and songwriters have walked away from the faith when their own strength finally crumbled, because the Scriptures alone didn't bring life? The Scriptures tell you where to find life and strength, but it is only through close relationship with Jesus you can experience it.

As I was tentatively dipping my toes into a less "religious" ideology, God showed me Jesus' words in John 5:39-44[A]:

> "You study the Scriptures diligently because you think that in them you have eternal life. These are the very Scriptures that testify about me, yet you refuse to come to me to have life. I do not accept glory from human beings, but I know you. I know that you do not have the love of God in your hearts."

Those words cut me to the core. I knew the Scriptures, but I wasn't experiencing the fullness of life and love God had for me. Jesus isn't saying the Scriptures are bad. He's just saying they won't give us eternal life in themselves. They point us to Jesus.

If we study the Scriptures and don't come to Jesus for life, we've missed it. I believed Jesus and knew I had eternal life, but I just couldn't figure out how to come to Him for that fullness of life that is available this side of heaven.

Jesus rarely condemned people, but when He did, it was the religious leaders. Matthew 3:7-8,10[D] says,

> But when he saw many of the Pharisees and Sadducees coming to his baptism, he said to them, "Brood of vipers! Who warned you to flee from the wrath to come? Therefore bear fruits worthy of repentance.... And even now the ax is laid to the root of the trees. Therefore every tree which does not bear good fruit is cut down and thrown into the fire."

Is your life bearing good fruit? My fruit was minimal and probably wouldn't have tasted good. In Matthew 23:23-28[C] Jesus says,

> "Woe to you, scribes and Pharisees, hypocrites! For you tithe mint and dill and cummin, and have neglected the weightier provisions of the law: justice and mercy and faithfulness; but these are the things you should have done without neglecting the others. You blind guides, who strain out a gnat and swallow a camel!

"Woe to you, scribes and Pharisees, hypocrites! For you clean the outside of the cup and of the dish, but inside they are full of robbery and self-indulgence. You blind Pharisee, first clean the inside of the cup and of the dish, so that the outside of it may become clean also.

"Woe to you, scribes and Pharisees, hypocrites! For you are like whitewashed tombs which on the outside appear beautiful, but inside they are full of dead men's bones and all uncleanness. So you, too, outwardly appear righteous to men, but inwardly you are full of hypocrisy and lawlessness."

Are you living in self-indulgence while appearing upright on the outside? Are you acting like you have abundant life, while feeling dead on the inside? Do you loudly declare the importance of morality and good works, while inside feeling like a slave to sin? If so, you are not alone. I was there. Sometimes I'm drawn back there, but now I know there is something more. So, I climb back out and into the freedom and victory of Christ!

I could go on comparing myself to the Pharisees, but for the sake of time, let's just make a quick list of further qualities Jesus calls out negatively in the Pharisees:

- They judge themselves as better for knowing the Scriptures (John 5:39)
- They do not produce good fruit (Matthew 23)
- They teach laws but do not follow them (Matthew 23)
- They love being honored more than doing right (Matthew 23)
- They pray long prayers to look more spiritual (Matthew 23)
- They are full of pride about their spiritual works (Luke 18)
- They care more about following God's rules than loving and helping people (Luke 13)
- They care more about church tradition than the law of God (Matthew 15)

- They honor God with their lips, but their hearts are far away from Him (Matthew 15)
- They teach the precepts of man as doctrine (Matthew 15)
- They judge people who spend time with sinners (Matthew 9)
- They care more about outward appearance than the inner heart (Matthew 23)

Do you see yourself in any of these? There is no condemnation here, but an offer of a better way. Let me reintroduce you to a man by the name of Nicodemus. John 3:1-2[C] says,

> *Now there was a man of the Pharisees, named Nicodemus, a ruler of the Jews; this man came to Jesus by night and said to Him, "Rabbi, we know that You have come from God as a teacher; for no one can do these signs that You do unless God is with him."*

As I have further pursued my journey into a more Spirit-led faith, I have repeatedly felt like Nicodemus. I kept thinking of people I knew who would be disconcerted by the direction my husband and I were headed in our faith.

I was seeing miraculous signs and good fruit like Nicodemus saw in Jesus, and I knew God was in those. Even so, I was concerned about how I would be judged for believing it. As a result, I didn't talk much about the things we were seeing. I wanted to be sure it was from God before I said anything, just as Nicodemus wanted to be sure, which was evidenced by his coming to talk to Jesus at night.

Most people will recognize the next verse, John 3:3[D], which says, "Jesus answered and said to him, 'Most assuredly, I say to you, unless one is born again, he cannot see the kingdom of God.'" The term "born again" became popular in the 1960s to refer to those who have had a conversion experience and are now "saved." Let's not forget the second part of the verse. We can now see the kingdom of God!

Continuing to John 3:4ᶜ, "Nicodemus said to Him, 'How can a man be born when he is old? He cannot enter a second time into his mother's womb and be born; can he?'"

Nicodemus hears what Jesus says and focuses on the "born again" part, asking about what it means. Again, I feel like I connect with Nicodemus here. What I'm learning these days is leading to so many questions. It's bringing up questions I had before—ones that I shoved down and covered up with whatever theology I had. Ones I felt would make me look uneducated if I asked. And now questions come up based on new experiences that conflict with my old theology.

Thankfully, I am at a church with pastors and other leaders who welcome and encourage questions and searching. And as usual, right now I have a list of things to ask when I next have time to reach out to our pastors.

Jesus, in true Jesus fashion, answered Nicodemus' question without fully answering the question. John 3:5-6ᴰ says, "Jesus answered, 'Most assuredly, I say to you, unless one is born of water and the Spirit, he cannot enter the kingdom of God. That which is born of the flesh is flesh, and that which is born of the Spirit is spirit.'"

I find this interesting since the evangelical community is the one that was first associated with the term "born again" and yet quite a few evangelicals I know would be pretty uncomfortable with, or even downright opposed to, some of the things I'm seeing the Holy Spirit do. I mostly believed that the Holy Spirit's role was to help change us so we sin less, convict and teach us when we read the Bible, and to occasionally answer our prayers when they are prayed with "if it's your will" at the end.

In John 3:7-8ᴮ, Jesus says, "Do not marvel that I said to you, 'You must be born again.' The wind blows where it wishes, and you hear its sound, but you do not know where it comes from or where it goes. So it is with everyone who is born of the Spirit."

I never truly understood this, and probably still don't fully. Jesus answers in riddles, and I have learned that this is an attempt to draw us in. Too often we feel it is to push us away. It seems also that in our earthly understanding, we just can't comprehend the Spirit. The wind/breath/spirit blows where it wishes. You can't control it.

Those who are Spirit-led look different, seem to be moving to a different drummer, not following the ways and methods of the world. Nicodemus is no less confused than I am. But he doesn't try to cover it up and hide behind his position as a leader and behind his education in the Scriptures. He wants to know so he risks another question. John 3:9-15[C] says,

> *Nicodemus said to Him, "How can these things be?" Jesus answered and said to him, "Are you the teacher of Israel and do not understand these things? Truly, truly, I say to you, we speak of what we know and testify of what we have seen, and you do not accept our testimony. If I told you earthly things and you do not believe, how will you believe if I tell you heavenly things? No one has ascended into heaven, but He who descended from heaven: the Son of Man. As Moses lifted up the serpent in the wilderness, even so must the Son of Man be lifted up; so that whoever believes will in Him have eternal life."*

We don't have Nicodemus' response to this. I'm sure this only brought up more questions. Whether he asked them or not, we don't have a record. Looking back, we understand Jesus is predicting His death on the cross and telling us how to have eternal life. His death and resurrection allow access to salvation and to His Spirit—who was sent to believers everywhere when He returned to the Father.

The next time we see Nicodemus in Scripture is in John 7:47-52[D],

> *Then the Pharisees answered them, "Are you also deceived? Have any of the rulers or the Pharisees believed in Him? But this crowd*

> *that does not know the law is accursed." Nicodemus (he who came to Jesus by night, being one of them) said to them, "Does our law judge a man before it hears him and knows what he is doing?" They answered and said to him, "Are you also from Galilee? Search and look, for no prophet has arisen out of Galilee."*

Nicodemus is starting to believe, but still holding back, being cautious, because those in his circles are strongly against these new teachings he's begun to believe. Again, I connect with him. As I started to believe some of the more miraculous things I saw, I was hesitant to share them with people who weren't comfortable with the idea. I was still processing everything and not ready to risk condemnation from people I admire and respect.

The final place we see Nicodemus is after the death of Jesus. I find it interesting that Jesus' twelve disciples are not there. But instead, two men, who were disciples in secret, risk being associated with the crucified Christ. John 19:38-42[c] says,

> *After these things Joseph of Arimathea, being a disciple of Jesus, but a secret one for fear of the Jews, asked Pilate that he might take away the body of Jesus; and Pilate granted permission. So he came and took away His body. Nicodemus, who had first come to Him by night, also came, bringing a mixture of myrrh and aloes, about a hundred pounds weight. So they took the body of Jesus and bound it in linen wrappings with the spices, as is the burial custom of the Jews. Now in the place where He was crucified there was a garden, and in the garden a new tomb in which no one had yet been laid. Therefore because of the Jewish day of preparation, since the tomb was nearby, they laid Jesus there.*

I wonder if it finally made sense to Nicodemus—the reference to the snake in the wilderness and the Son of Man having to be "lifted up." Had he been turning those words over in his mind since that first night?

Pharisee Set Free

Whether he understood the fullness of what had just happened or not, I hope he continued to step out in faith. In Acts 15:5, we do find out that there was a group of Pharisees who believed and were part of the early church. It's possible that Nicodemus was one of their leaders.

Speaking of Pharisees who were part of the early church, a chapter on Pharisees would be incomplete without looking at everyone's favorite Pharisee turned believer—Saul (aka Paul).

The first time we meet Saul in the end of Acts 7 and beginning of chapter 8, he is watching the stoning of Stephen and approving of it. Shortly thereafter, in Acts 8:3[B], we read, "But Saul was ravaging the church, and entering house after house, he dragged off men and women and committed them to prison."

He says about his past in Philippians 3:4b-6[A],

> *If someone else thinks they have reasons to put confidence in the flesh, I have more: circumcised on the eighth day, of the people of Israel, of the tribe of Benjamin, a Hebrew of Hebrews; in regard to the law, a Pharisee; as for zeal, persecuting the church; as for righteousness based on the law, faultless.*

Some in the church place confidence in their moral successes, in never having taken part in the vices of the culture, in living up to such a high standard. They believe they must be worth more in the eyes of God. Some like to talk about their discipline of always having quiet times and prayer, as if those things move you a step up the spiritual ladder, and of all the ways they have served the church. They find their value in their successes.

Certainly, all these things are good and important, but they are the wrong place to put your value. Because if you have one moral failure, then you no longer have value. If you start missing quiet times, there goes your value. Make one of the big moral mistakes, and you begin to wonder if

God still loves you. I have good news if you feel that way—your value to God is not in any of these things. Keep reading.

Paul had such a profound encounter with God that he knew none of his past credentials or works mattered. He goes on in Philippians 3:7-9a[E], saying,

> *I once thought these things were valuable, but now I consider them worthless because of what Christ has done. Yes, everything else is worthless when compared with the infinite value of knowing Christ Jesus my Lord. For his sake I have discarded everything else, counting it all as garbage, so that I could gain Christ and become one with him. I no longer count on my own righteousness through obeying the law; rather, I become righteous through faith in Christ.*

I did not understand this passion in Paul that pulled at him to know God more and more, to be so done with who he was in the past. I had not yet come to a place where I didn't mind letting go of every part of who I was so I could be more like Jesus. I did not understand being ready to take risks to attain all that Christ purchased for me in His resurrection from the dead. I did not understand until I had my own encounters with God's goodness and His power.

As long as we think we have value in things outside of Christ and feel like we are doing good enough, we will be afraid to let go of that person we see ourselves as. We will fear that God might change the small part of us that we like and value.

Paul goes on to say in Philippians 3:12-13[A], "Not that I have already obtained all this...But one thing I do: Forgetting what is behind and straining toward what is ahead..."

This passage moves me so deeply these days. I often feel that same desire to strain ahead taking hold of me. I know that desire is something

I didn't produce in myself, but it is a result of God in me. A whole lot of transformation had to happen for me to get to this point, and that's what we'll cover next.

But first, it's your turn to take a moment to reflect on your past, your journey, your present, and your future.

1. What stood out to you in this chapter on Pharisees? What is God saying to you?

2. Have you ever wondered if you were a Pharisee? Why?

3. What characteristics do you share with the Pharisees?

4. Where do you find your value? Is that a good place to put your value?

5. When have you experienced God in a life-changing way? If you haven't, would you want to experience God in that way?

6. What fruit of the Spirit are being produced in your life?

7. In what ways do you identify with Nicodemus?

8. In what ways do you identify with Paul?

CHAPTER 3

Theology Versus Faith

For I resolved to know nothing while I was with you except Jesus Christ and him crucified.

- 1 Corinthians 2:2[A]

Theology at its core is a good thing. Merriam Webster dictionary defines *theology* as "the study of religious faith, practice, and experience… especially: the study of God and of God's relation to the world." (Retrieved February 12, 2020, from https://www.merriam-webster.com/theology)

It is an important part of Christianity—studying God's Word and getting to know who God is and how He relates to us. But the word *theology* also has a nuance of being very academic and impersonal.

As I matured in my Christian walk, I began to think theology was a critical part of the Christian life. Looking back, I may have unconsciously elevated it above faith. Theology wants to study, explain, and understand God and His nature. Faith is not so concerned with explanation and evidence but relates to having confidence in where we place our hope. Hebrews 11:6a[A] says, "without faith it is impossible to please God."

I had built a whole lot of theology to explain how all the confusing parts of Scripture fit together and how Scripture fit with my life experiences. And I'd believed a whole lot of theology based on other people's experiences. I'd cried and wrestled with God over many core issues when I took a Christian doctrine class in college. And in the end, I had found a way for them all to fit together and not fall over... most of the time.

I thought these theologies, backed up with Scripture, made me educated, close to God, and secure in my faith. I privately felt prideful about my knowledge of Scripture and theology. Sure, I had some tiny nagging concerns when I read about the Pharisees and the importance of producing fruit, but everyone around me—including those whom I considered much more educated than myself—seemed to think, believe, and behave mostly as I did.

Don't misunderstand me. I'll reiterate—I was saved and knew God and loved God. I understood that I needed heart knowledge, not just head knowledge. By the time I finished college, I recognized that I was coming out of a legalistic mindset. I was slowly moving forward and making progress to become less legalistic. But because my view of who God was hadn't changed from that of a Father who was overly concerned with my moral behavior and less concerned about pretty much everything else, I didn't fully make it out.

One of the major topics in the Christian church is sin, and for good reason. What we believe about sin and how we deal with sin is an important part of the Christian life. There are two extremes in the church when dealing with sin. One side is all about grace—focusing on how we are not under the law and how God will forgive us. The other side is all about morality and killing sin and looking down on the other side for overemphasizing grace. Paul addresses some of this in Romans 6:1-2D, "What shall we say then? Shall we continue in sin that grace may abound? Certainly not! How shall we who died to sin live any longer in it?"

Those who like to quote this verse say that the most important thing in our Christian life is to avoid sin. For years, Christian circles have set up boundaries to help us avoid falling into sin. This is especially true in areas like sexual purity. The teaching around sexual purity can often look like the teachings of the Pharisees in the time of the Jews, adding extra rules in order to avoid breaking the actual law.

Unfortunately, because such emphasis is placed on sexual purity, a lot of people who fall into this type of sin feel they cannot come clean without harsh judgement, and they fall for the lie that God no longer loves them. Sadly, many of the leaders that teach most passionately against sexual sin also end up being the ones who then end up falling into that temptation.

I'm not saying churches shouldn't preach against sexual sin, I'm just saying adding all the extra layers of rules and placing so much emphasis on it has driven people away from God rather than to God, because they feel their worth is connected to their purity. Paul goes on to say in Romans 6:14^C, "For sin shall not be master over you, for you are not under law but under grace." Many who quote Romans 6:1-2 can struggle with feeling like sin is still a master over them.

The most powerful thing I've learned about sin lately is how God actually views it. We've been told over and over that God the Father cannot stand sin (or at least that's the lesson I learned). I learned that sin separates us from God. This is true, but this is because we have stepped away from Him. It is not Him stepping away from us.

When we look up and find ourselves far from God in our heart, we are the ones who have moved. It's not Him leaving as a response to our sin. We don't need to clean ourselves up before going back to God. God isn't hiding from us when we sin, or waiting for us to do penance, or shaming us, or condemning us.

Jesus, who perfectly reflects the Father's heart, doesn't condemn a single person who comes to Him honestly seeking. We even see Him sharing meals with those considered the worst sinners. Instead, Jesus only condemns the religious leaders who have set up extra rules to keep themselves from sin, but whose hearts were far from God.

I've read Genesis more times than I can count. But when someone finally pointed out to me how God responds to Adam and Eve after they sinned in the garden, I took a step back from my theological mindset and was amazed at how incorrect I'd been. The account in Genesis 3 shows Adam and Eve eating the fruit. God knows they have eaten the fruit, but He still shows up at the normal time to take a walk with them in the cool of the day.

He doesn't send an angel to tell them, "Sorry guys, God can't talk to you since you sinned. Here's your punishment. Now get out." He doesn't just show up to punish them and then leave. He comes and talks with them. He does tell them the consequences of their actions, but then He stays and makes them clothes (Genesis 3:21). He Himself took a living animal, sacrificed it, and from the animal's skin made them clothes. And then, in His mercy, He banished them from the garden.

He knew that since they now had the knowledge of good and evil, and now that sin had entered the picture, they could not be allowed to eat of the fruit of the tree of life or they would live forever in their sin—forever in a fallen and evil world. He needed to first redeem us before we would be allowed to taste the tree of life again. Even then, God didn't abandon them. We see specifically that God still speaks to Cain, has a relationship with Enoch, and talked with Noah.

I didn't realize God wants me to come to Him after I sin. I felt like I needed to do a lot of repenting and stay away until the shame left. This is one of the great deceptions that has permeated Christian circles today. We feel guilt that should lead us back to God, but instead we let it turn to shame that keeps us away from God.

A friend recently asked me to share my thoughts relating to how a prominent Spirit-led group seems to ignore sin in the teaching and worship they release. I haven't studied this movement's material in depth, so I couldn't speak to it one way or the other. But, I explained some of what I

Theology Versus Faith

had been learning about sin that might explain that movement's seeming silence regarding the topic.

You see, counter to what you might thing, the more people focus their mental energies on not sinning, the more they seem to sin, and the more discouraged they become. Whereas the more people focus on praising God and being in His presence, the less they are inclined to be tempted to sin. This is likely why that movement seems to speak less about sin and more about seeking God's presence—because being in God's presence makes sin less appealing.

When I was younger, I learned that God had defeated sin and that, as a Christian, I was no longer a slave to it. So why, I wondered, did I still feel like I was? Why did I still have to work so hard not to sin? If God defeated sin, I shouldn't have to struggle. But that was not my reality.

Now, the more time I spend with God and in His presence, the less I desire to sin. And when I don't desire to sin, I don't have to work so hard to resist it. So why does the church put the cart before the horse? Why don't they teach you to focus on and love being in God's presence before demanding that you be perfect?

The typical church is a place full of people wearing a mask of perfection. Sure, in Bible study groups we may have vulnerable moments. But even when people seem to open up, we sometimes find it was just the tip of an iceberg whose true size is only revealed when their mess becomes public (as we've seen happen far too often). Only then do we realize just how much people try to hide.

The culture we live in now is one that allows no failure. One photo or video or even the testimony of one accuser (true or not) can destroy a person. And while we are called to live a life above reproach, this has created a place where people are afraid to bring their sin into the light and repent. And we find that people are still failing by the millions.

I mentioned that when we started looking for a new church, one of my biggest concerns was not being led astray. I didn't want fine sounding arguments to sway me from the truth. We came out of a group of churches whose ideology I still greatly respect. I love their passion for the Word of God, for not leaving anything out, and for knowing the truth.

I am so thankful for my grounding in Scripture from my parents' teaching, from growing up in the church, from going to Christian schools where I studied the Bible in class, and from being at churches that were passionate about teaching the Word of God. That grounding in Scripture has given me the deep roots that have allowed such growth in this new season of faith.

It also had the side effect of making me concerned about, and perhaps even judgmental of, churches that only had one or two verses in the entire sermon. But, as we visited dozens of churches near us, I noticed truth was being taught at all of them. Some in more depth than others, but all were teaching truth.

Our first few months at our new church were interesting. We knew God had brought us to this specific church for this season. We knew and loved that God's presence was there on Sunday mornings. We liked that the pastor taught from the Bible and spent a lot of time in Scripture. But, it was also one of the more uncomfortable churches we'd been in, because there were things said and done that were outside our normal. And those things pushed uncomfortably against all that theology I'd built.

I'd like to point out again that no church will have everything perfectly right. I've heard it said that if you are looking for a church that is perfect in every way, make sure you are perfect before you attend so you don't ruin it. Just because the pastor is exactly right about one topic or passage doesn't mean that they are one hundred percent right about everything else. Or just because God's presence shows up in worship doesn't mean that God condones everything that happens in the service.

Theology Versus Faith

Our faith shouldn't rest solely on what one pastor or one church says. Rather, it should rest on what the Bible says. We are so incredibly blessed to be able to read (and understand with the help of the Holy Spirit) the Scriptures for ourselves, in a language we know, without threat to our lives. You can read it for yourself! And it's our responsibility to search the Scriptures to see if what we are learning is in line with what God's Word says.

It was helpful that many people in our church, including the pastors, came out of religious backgrounds that were similar to ours. Many had even come from a place of similar theology. Many had been hurt in the past by the church. But instead of leaving the church (or after God brought them back from time away from the church) and blaming God, they pressed in to see who God really is.

As I look at my friends and well-known Christians who are leaving the faith, I recognize that there are major problems facing the church today. I would submit that the theology they've been taught and the church family itself have let them down, because they both represent God poorly. The church no longer operates as a body, so the members (arms and legs and fingers) aren't getting what they need.

Those who are leaving the church see the problem, but not the source of the problem. Instead, they simply abandon Christianity. They decide to leave in search of something that will make them feel loved, seen, accepted, valuable, and powerful, without realizing that was what Jesus wanted to do for them all along. The problem isn't Christianity, it's that many of us have contorted God and faith and the Christian life into something far less than what it's intended to be, filled with half-truths and sometimes outright lies.

One Sunday our pastor talked about theologies we build based on experiences in our lives. He asked us to just momentarily imagine setting a specific theology on a shelf, and to honestly look at what the Bible says and who God is. In retrospect, this moment was a turning point in my walk with God. I realized that, without discarding my theology or changing my mind, I could take a step back and examine it.

You'd think, after being in a doctrine class in college, I'd have learned this was okay, but something about that being an academic exercise and this being a spiritual practice made it feel different. I wasn't letting deception in, but rather reexamining why I believed what I believed. I was checking Scripture to see if it really did line up, and deciding whether to take the theology back on, adjust it a little so it better fit Scripture, leave it on the shelf for a time, or completely discard it as wrong.

This practice was so freeing that I decided to set not just one, but most of my theologies on the shelf for examination. If they were true, there was no risk in looking at them critically. Honestly, I allowed myself a lot of time to look at them. I have finally decided to discard a couple of theologies that I now see cannot be biblical. Others I've taken back on because I see that they are in line with Scripture. Some theologies have been tweaked slightly because they were just a little off. The rest I still have on a shelf full of theologies, waiting to see how they measure up. Doing this let me start anew, searching the Scriptures, talking to God, asking questions that in the past I would have thought I was far too spiritually superior to ask.

By separating myself from these theologies and metaphorically setting them on a shelf, I was able to see them more clearly. I could better examine the weight and shape of them. In doing so, I realized that my first problem, as we've discussed, was that I had my theologies stacked incorrectly. I had smaller, less important, and even slightly incorrect theologies on the foundation, which caused more important theologies to become unstable and need extra propping up in order to stay balanced.

For example, I had a theology that God gave people bad experiences to help them grow closer to Him. So, I also had a theology (fear) that God would make something bad happen to me to help me grow closer to Him. I kept waiting for some major negative life event to happen.

This theology was based on the fact that bad things happen to Christians all the time. And it was based on another theology that, since God was in control of everything that happens and actively coordinating everything, He also must be the author of everything.

This, along with other theologies, made me doubt God's goodness. Actually, it made me think I needed to redefine the words *good* and *love*, since my God, who was good and loving, gave people bad experiences or at the very least allowed these things for our benefit.

It was pointed out to me that people who allow bad things to happen to other people are never seen as good, and, in reality, can be prosecuted for crimes. If you know someone is abusing a person, especially if you are in authority over them, you have an obligation to act or you are an accomplice to the crime. You are not considered "good" for allowing those being harmed to suffer so they can grow stronger. Ezekiel 34:2b-4[c] says,

> *Thus says the Lord God, "Woe, shepherds of Israel who have been feeding themselves! Should not the shepherds feed the flock? You eat the fat and clothe yourselves with the wool, you slaughter the fat sheep without feeding the flock. Those who are sickly you have not strengthened, the diseased you have not healed, the broken you have not bound up, the scattered you have not brought back, nor have you sought for the lost; but with force and with severity you have dominated them."*

God condemns the shepherds who allow and overlook the bad things that happen to the flock, which is symbolic of His people.

The theology that "God allows bad things to happen so He can bring about good" was closely connected to my theology about God being in control.

But since I needed to put everything on the shelf, both theologies went there together as I searched for answers to my tough questions. In what ways does God orchestrate everything and in what ways does He allow the world to go the way it is going and wait for us to bring His will to earth? In what ways is God trying to get us, as co-laborers, to participate in stopping the bad things that are happening as a result of sin and decay and death existing in the world?

Ezekiel 22:30[B] says, "And I sought for a man among them who should build up the wall and stand in the breach before me for the land, that I should not destroy it, but I found none."

And Isaiah 6:8[D] says, "Also I heard the voice of the Lord, saying: 'Whom shall I send, And who will go for Us?' Then I said, 'Here am I! Send me.'"

In Ephesians 2:10[B] Paul writes, "For we are his workmanship, created in Christ Jesus for good works, which God prepared beforehand, that we should walk in them."

It seems that God gives us guidance and direction—in the old covenant from the law and the prophets, and in the New Testament from Scriptures and the Holy Spirit. But outside of these and the natural laws and consequences He put in place, the world mostly goes the way mankind chooses, with God's main (but not only) way of intervention being through His people. He acts in response to our intercession and prayers. And He also speaks to people to guide them in what to do as His body and representatives here on Earth.

He is not planning out difficult things to give us, but rather looking for people who will partner with Him and bring His good and perfect will to earth through their prayers, actions, and faith. He sees the horrible world events (that come as a result of living in a fallen world) before they arrive. He speaks to us to intercede to prevent them or minimize the damage and to be His light as well as His hands and feet in the midst

Theology Versus Faith

of the darkness. But so often we are distracted or haven't ever learned to distinguish His voice from all the other noise.

I imagine quite a few people, many who are more educated and influential than I am, will really dislike what I've just said. The theology that God foreordains or allows bad things in our lives has permeated the church. I would submit that if you really consider some of the bad things in the world, you won't be able to attribute them to God and still believe in His goodness.

For example, look at the well-known example of the abuse within the Catholic Church. People in higher positions of authority turned a blind eye to the abuse they had knowledge of. They ignored the fact that local priests were abusing people and children who were under their authority. Was that God's will? Was it His will that those people and children be abused by someone representing Him? Was it His will that those in higher places of authority in the church overlook the abuse that was happening? Does God willingly allow abuse within the church to make people stronger?

I submit that He does not. It is the enemy who comes to destroy. God hates what happened. Jesus' passion when He went in the temple and turned over all those money tables—that is how He feels when people who represent Him do harm to those in their care. His heart breaks over that.

So, the next question is *why*. Why doesn't God stop it? If He doesn't stop it, does that mean He allows it? (We'll look more at that in chapter ten.) Why didn't He step in, back in the Garden of Eden, when it all went wrong to begin with? Why did He put the tree of good and evil in the garden? Did He not know all the pain that would come?

I do not have all the answers, and I won't until I'm in heaven and all has been revealed. Please beware of anyone who claims to have all the answers. I am also a work in progress. I'm so thankful for how far I've come. I hope and pray that every day I grow closer to the heart of God, that I continue being perfected and grow to know Him more deeply and hear Him more clearly every day.

But, as I was searching, God showed me something powerful about the tree in the garden. What the tree in the garden means is that God values freedom much more than we in the church do. Why does He love freedom? Because it is the only way to have a genuine relationship.

If the purpose of the Christian life was to just be good, moral people and to tell people about God so they could also become good, moral people, then He wouldn't have put that tree in the garden. He had perfect people. But without the tree of the knowledge of good and evil, they had no ability to choose Him and love Him.

For a time, I believed I had no ability to choose Him. I was taught the basics of Calvinism from people who were strong believers and knew and loved God dearly. I do not discount their faith or relationship with the Lord. If you consider yourself a Calvinist, please don't stop reading. This is my faith journey—it doesn't have to be yours—but perhaps it will help you understand those with a different theology.

Predestination, as a theology, generally means that God chooses those He wants and doesn't choose others. The theology of predestination bothered me for many years. The idea that God chooses some people, and because of irresistible grace they cannot reject God's choosing, seems to go completely against having a tree of the knowledge of good and evil in the garden. I submit that you cannot have a real relationship with someone who has forced you to choose them. You can only have Stockholm syndrome.

It may sound odd, but now the tree of the knowledge of good and evil represents "hope" to me. God, knowing full well what would happen, still put it there. It is like an engagement ring. He put it there and got down on one knee and said, "I want you to be my bride. Please choose me." In the love story that is the Bible—the story of God pursuing us—He's been asking us to choose Him.

I had a major emotional breakdown after finishing my Christian doctrine class in college. I was in an environment where most people believed strongly in predestination. I was in a family of Presbyterians (historically). As a teenager growing in my faith, I'd always leaned more toward semi-Pelagianism, which in general terms means we have a choice whether we respond to God's grace and follow Him. My breakdown came because it was made clear to me in doctrine class that, if I believed the Bible was true, I had to believe in predestination because there was enough Scripture to back it up.

I broke down in tears over this in the weeks and months afterwards because I didn't understand. If God was love and if He desires that none should perish, how could He have predestined only some to be saved, which meant He predestined some to not be saved. I wrestled for months. But finally, because I'd been persuaded that it was scriptural, I told God something along the lines of, "I'll love you, but only because you forced me to."

Thankfully, I had someone speak into my life and show me another way to understand and believe the Scriptures that speak of predestination, without accepting the theology of predestination. This even happened prior to our switching churches. Certainly, we can only choose Him because He chose us first. However, I'd like you to consider the possibility that God chooses all, but values each one's free will to choose Him back. 1 Timothy 2:3-4[B] says, "This is good, and it is pleasing in the sight of God our Savior, who desires all people to be saved and to come to the knowledge of the truth."

Even so, the new revelation I had about God putting the tree in the garden gave me so much hope. I felt so loved. And it showed me how I'd gotten it wrong as a mom. Because if I had a choice with my kids, I'd have been tempted to not put a tree there. My theology was even affecting the way I parented my kids. And let me tell you, nothing makes me want to get rid of bad theology like realizing how it will affect my kids.

By putting all these theologies on the shelf and reexamining them, I was able to put the most critical and the most biblical theologies back where they belonged. God loves us. Jesus died to redeem us. He is the way, the truth, and the life. God is good—all the time. If a theology I examine makes God no longer good or loving, it will need to be reexamined.

Now, I still need to be careful to define *good* and *love* the way the Bible defines them. I can't just say this is what love means to me. I need to see how Jesus showed love. We need to examine what the Bible says about God before making any further theologies, and we will do that in the chapters ahead.

For the moment, I'm stepping back from the idea of having a theology and into the idea of just having faith. We've had quite a few experiences in our new church related to the more miraculous gifts of the Spirit. Instead of focusing on placing all the new experiences into a theology, I'm returning to the basics. I want to just be with God and look at who He is in Scripture with fresh eyes.

I have experienced His presence in greater measure, heard His voice more consistently and profoundly, seen things straight out of Acts that I didn't think were for today. I have more peace, joy, love—all the fruits of the Spirit. I'm no longer uncertain about heaven. Before, I knew I'd go to heaven, but I just wasn't sure what that would be like. Would we all just sing songs forever?

I knew God was going to still weigh all the things we'd done on earth, even if we had Jesus to get us in. That sounded scary. While I should still hold God in reverent fear, realizing that He is not an angry and disappointed

Theology Versus Faith

father helps me better respond to His love and to anticipate the glorious moment when I get to be with Him in heaven.

Understanding God the Father correctly was another huge turning point in the journey. He is not an angry father who is just waiting to punish us, who has only been held back by Jesus' mercy. Whether you had a good father or not, you likely shape your view of God the Father based on your view of your own father, or your view of the leaders in your church. Colossians 1:12-15[D] says,

> *Giving thanks to the Father who has qualified us to be partakers of the inheritance of the saints in the light. He has delivered us from the power of darkness and conveyed us into the kingdom of the Son of His love, in whom we have redemption through His blood, the forgiveness of sins. He is the image of the invisible God, the firstborn over all creation.*

God the Father is the one who delivered us from the power of darkness and brought us into the kingdom of the Son He loves. Jesus only did what He saw His Father doing and said what He heard His Father saying (John 15:19). God the Father loves you with an everlasting love, far better than any human father could love you. If you find that hard to believe, ask yourself why? Why don't I think God is a better father than any human father? Then ask God to prove you wrong.

My theology was based on both my experiences and my lack of experiences. I thought it was based on the Bible. Now that I've stopped focusing on theology, I've seen the Bible come to life. Some of my experiences now point to a new theology, but I'm not going to make anything a theology just because of an experience. I'm going to see what God is doing and make sure it is God by testing it against the Bible and the fruit it brings.

I didn't often see God move under my old theology. Probably because I'd given Him so many reasons not to, and I didn't really expect Him to.

Sure, I'd hope and pray He would do something, but I really didn't believe that was His heart toward me. Now I see God move regularly because I'm in a church that believes He wants to move and sets up areas where God must show up or they look like failures. I used to think looking like a failure was the worst possible scenario. Now I see that the worst scenario is missing God because I'm too afraid to fail.

The presence of God changed me. The voice of God changed me. The heart of God changed me. I still regularly get caught in a mental battle of theologies at times (quite a few times writing this chapter), but I have people who help me take a step back and find Jesus again. There is so much Scripture that pushes against other parts of Scripture, and before we can deal with it, we need to know who God is and who we are in Christ. We will press into that in the next few chapters.

So now it's your turn.

1. What did God highlight to you in this chapter on theology? How is your experience similar to or different from mine?

2. What experiences in life have formed some of your theologies? If you were to put those theologies on the shelf in order to examine if they are really in line with Scripture, what do you think would be the result?

3. What truth in Scripture is hardest to fit into your current belief system?

4. What do you do with Scriptures that don't seem to fit?

5. How often do you see God moving in your current belief system?

6. How do you handle the problem of sin? Are you living in the victory Jesus won or constantly striving hard in your own effort to gain victory over sin?

7. How has your theology changed over time? As you consider this chapter, do you feel the change was for better or for worse?

8. Do you get stuck like I do in a theological vortex of battling ideas? How do you escape it?

CHAPTER 4

Encountering God

"I love those who love me, and those who seek me diligently find me."

- Proverbs 8:17[B]

People can study the Scripture without ever really encountering God. Plenty of atheists and agnostics have read more of the Bible than many Christians have. Without the Holy Spirit, we have no hope of understanding God's Word, and without encountering God, we cannot hope to be changed.

I can think of times throughout my life when I encountered God. I remember, while in high school, coming home from a mission trip and feeling so depressed. I had been on this spiritual high, worshiping passionately every day, encountering God, and then I was back to reality. I was warned by other Christians not to chase spiritual highs. They were few and far between and, if you chased them, you'd always be disappointed.

I was told that I shouldn't base my faith on feeling God's presence, but on the truth that He is there. While this advice isn't wrong, it is also not completely true. God's Holy Spirit comes to live within us when we are saved. God is omnipresent—there is nowhere on earth or in heaven you can run from God's presence. But we are also told that God rewards those who seek Him (Hebrews 11:6). I settled for seeking God's hand when I should have been seeking His face.

The first morning I stepped foot into what would eventually become our church home, I knew I was someplace special. There were many wonderful things that drew me in. However, the aspect that most stood out was that, standing there worshiping, I truly felt like I was experiencing a small taste of heaven. That experience is because God showed up. His Spirit was there that morning in a way that was beyond His omnipresent presence and beyond the presence He promises when two or three are gathered. His presence is felt there pretty much every Sunday morning.

I'd privately wondered about heaven for many years. I thought it seemed a little boring if all we did forever was worship God. That false belief was a result of worshiping Him without knowing His presence. His presence changes everything.

We should not chase feelings. They ebb and flow. We will have spiritual seasons and times when we cling to God because we know He is there, even if we don't feel it. But we should chase God's presence. I have had plenty of seasons in my life where I had a quiet time because I knew I should, so I did it whether I felt like it or not. There were seasons I didn't have one at all and felt guilty. Currently, I crave my quiet time with God most days because I'm learning to be in His presence, even when I'm not at church.

His presence isn't about an emotional feeling, though it can be experienced that way. His presence is simply you being fully present with Him, and His focused presence toward you in response. It was His plan for us from the beginning. Now, with His spirit in us, He is always with us, but we are not always present with Him. It's up to you to choose to be present with God.

The thing about our church is that almost everyone shows up wanting to be in God's presence. That corporate desire to be present with God seems to allow us to experience His presence in greater measure. And once you've experienced it, once you've been made aware of it, you can

Encountering God

pursue it through relationship. I hope you will realize, like I did, that there is nothing better than being in the presence of God.

Before I had really experienced the presence of God, I'd obviously never known I could seek it out. I think a part of me was even a bit afraid of God's presence. Actually, part of me still is. I know that even in the moments when I experience God's presence, it is not the full weight of His presence.

I consider Isaiah's experience in Isaiah 6:1-5[D] an example of what it might be to experience more of the full weight of God's presence. He says,

> *In the year that King Uzziah died, I saw the Lord sitting on a throne, high and lifted up, and the train of His robe filled the temple. Above it stood seraphim; each one had six wings: with two he covered his face, with two he covered his feet, and with two he flew. And one cried to another and said: "Holy, holy, holy is the Lord of hosts; The whole earth is full of His glory!"*
>
> *And the posts of the door were shaken by the voice of him who cried out, and the house was filled with smoke. So I said: "Woe is me, for I am undone! Because I am a man of unclean lips, And I dwell in the midst of a people of unclean lips; For my eyes have seen the King, The Lord of hosts."*

I always wanted God to be safe. And by safe, I mean both comfortable and providing a bubble of protection so no physical, emotional, mental, or spiritual hurts could get to me. As a result, I was always powerfully challenged by the line in *The Lion, The Witch and The Wardrobe* by C.S. Lewis (1994) which says about Aslan (an allegory for Christ),

> *"Aslan is a lion- the Lion, the great Lion." "Ooh" said Susan. "I'd thought he was a man. Is he-quite safe? I shall feel rather nervous about meeting a lion."..."Safe?" said Mr Beaver..."Who said anything*

57

> *about safe? 'Course he isn't safe. But he's good. He's the King, I tell you." (p. 79-80).*

This is an allegory of what Scripture says about God. He's not "safe" in the way we might want. God's glory, holiness, and majesty are so far outside our earthly experience, there is no way to come before Him and feel anything other than exposed in every way and lacking any worth from ourselves—tempted to hide in fear.

But, even as we recognize that God will never fit in our comfort zone, we can also trust that God is good. Mark 10:18[C] says, "And Jesus said to him, 'Why do you call Me good? No one is good except God alone.'" I'd always thought I believed that God was good. I knew that was what Scripture said. I knew that God was holy, righteous, morally good, and perfect in every way. But somehow, I'd never fully believed in His ongoing goodness towards us.

I knew many specific verses about God's goodness, such as James 1:17[A], which says, "Every good and perfect gift is from above, coming down from the Father of the heavenly lights, who does not change like shifting shadows." And Psalm 145:9[A] which says, "The Lord is good to all; he has compassion on all he has made." But for some reason, I was under the impression that God's goodness towards us was based on our actions.

Sure, theologically I knew and claimed I believed that God loved me just as much while I was still separated from Him as He does when I do good things. But as I said before, I kept expecting God to hurt me or someone I loved as an act of "goodness" to teach me a lesson or draw me closer to Him. The first time I heard the song "Good Good Father" I felt like sobbing. I really needed reassurance. But even playing that song repeatedly didn't fully suppress my fear that God's goodness might be unpleasant.

Matthew 7:9-11[D] really speaks to people who feel the way I did. It reassures us that God is so much better than we expect. It says, "Or what man is there among you who, if his son asks for bread, will give him a stone? Or if he asks for a fish, will he give him a serpent? If you then, being evil, know how to give good gifts to your children, how much more will your Father who is in heaven give good things to those who ask Him!"

If you've grown up in church or been in church for a long time, you will know a whole lot about God, just like I did. I have heard about who God is all my life. But even so, I needed to let go of everything else that entangled me and return to the Word to really examine who God says He is, and decide if I truly believe it.

Would you be willing, just for the rest of this chapter, to set your beliefs on a shelf and ask God for discernment? The rest of the chapter is simply examining some of the other characteristics of God as stated in the Bible. I believe this will be helpful because sometimes we miss or gloss over parts of who God is because they press against one of the beliefs we've formed from a certain experience. Read on when you are ready.

God is love

If you have a way to listen to Isaiah 43:1-4[F] being read to you by an app on your phone or computer, take a moment to listen to it. If not, read it thoughtfully below. I've included the Message translation, but other versions are also powerful.

> *But now, God's Message,*
>   *the God who made you in the first place, Jacob,*
>   *the One who got you started, Israel:*
> *"Don't be afraid, I've redeemed you.*
>   *I've called your name. You're mine.*
> *When you're in over your head, I'll be there with you.*
>   *When you're in rough waters, you will not go down.*
> *When you're between a rock and a hard place,*

> *it won't be a dead end—*
> *Because I am God, your personal God,*
>   *The Holy of Israel, your Savior.*
> *I paid a huge price for you:*
>   *all of Egypt, with rich Cush and Seba thrown in!*
> *That's how much you mean to me!*
>   *That's how much I love you!*
> *I'd sell off the whole world to get you back,*
>   *trade the creation just for you."*

God's love for His people has been woven through history. And we as Christians are part of His people. He loves us! The Bible is filled with the truth that God is love.

- "Though the mountains be shaken and the hills be removed, yet my unfailing love for you will not be shaken nor my covenant of peace be removed," says the Lord, who has compassion on you. - Isaiah 54:10[A]

- For God so [greatly] loved and dearly prized the world, that He [even] gave His [One and] only begotten Son, so that whoever believes and trusts in Him [as Savior] shall not perish, but have eternal life. - John 3:16[G]

- But God demonstrates His own love toward us, in that while we were still sinners, Christ died for us. - Romans 5:8[D]

- Give thanks to the God of heaven, for his steadfast love endures forever. - Psalm 136:26[B]

- But God, being rich in mercy, because of His great love with which He loved us, even when we were dead in our transgressions, made us alive together with Christ (by grace you have been saved) - Ephesians 2:4-5[C]

- What marvelous love the Father has extended to us! Just look at it—we're called children of God! That's who we really are. But that's also why the world doesn't recognize us or take us seriously, because it has no idea who he is or what he's up to. - 1 John 3:1[F]

I could fill this chapter with all the verses that talk about God's love for us. 1 John 4:8[E] says "God is love." He is the embodiment of love. But we also need to look at how the Bible defines love.

We will, of course, be looking at 1 Corinthians 13:4-8[G] and, though you are probably familiar with it, please read it through and consider if you believe God loves you in this way.

> *Love endures with patience and serenity, love is kind and thoughtful, and is not jealous or envious; love does not brag and is not proud or arrogant. It is not rude; it is not self-seeking, it is not provoked [nor overly sensitive and easily angered]; it does not take into account a wrong endured. It does not rejoice at injustice, but rejoices with the truth [when right and truth prevail]. Love bears all things [regardless of what comes], believes all things [looking for the best in each one], hopes all things [remaining steadfast during difficult times], endures all things [without weakening].*
>
> *Love never fails [it never fades nor ends]. But as for prophecies, they will pass away; as for tongues, they will cease; as for the gift of special knowledge, it will pass away.*

Do you believe God truly loves you? Not you as part of a group of other people—you by yourself. Do you believe He loves you always and no matter what you've done? Even when you were dead in transgressions? Do you believe He loves you the way love is defined in 1 Corinthians 13?

If you are in doubt, I encourage you to continue to meditate on these Scriptures. Take time to search for even more Scriptures about His love for you. Join us again when you've let Him fill you up with the love He has for you.

God is for us

God is unequivocally with you and for you. Think of the people who took this to heart in the Bible. David stands out as one who stood with this expectation when he fought Goliath. In fact, in Psalm 118:6[C] the author who is believed to be David says, "The LORD is for me; I will not fear; What can man do to me?" How powerful this could be in our lives if we lived like we believed it.

Romans 8:31[E] says, "What shall we say about such wonderful things as these? If God is for us, who can ever be against us?"

He delights in us

We already looked at how God loves us, but the idea that God delights in us goes even above what many would believe about the way He loves us. Zephaniah 3:17[D] says, "The Lord your God in your midst, The Mighty One, will save; He will rejoice over you with gladness, He will quiet you with His love, He will rejoice over you with singing."

There is certainly a difference between loving and delighting in. I love my children always. I love them with every fiber of my being. I do not love them nearly as well as God loves me, but I love them as best I can. And I try to remember, even in the hard times, that it is important for them to know I like them as well as love them.

But I certainly don't always delight in them. In the moments when they are having a massive tantrum, I can still love them, but I've never found myself feeling delight in that moment. Now when they do the sweetest things, or even just when they are calm and I look in their faces, then I feel that overwhelming delight.

God's delight is not confined to a moment as a human parent's delight often is. He sees us as we will be and delights in us throughout the journey. That verse says He actually *rejoices over us with singing*.

He rewards those who seek Him

Hebrews 11:6^G says, "But without faith it is impossible to [walk with God and] please Him, for whoever comes [near] to God must [necessarily] believe that God exists and that He rewards those who [earnestly and diligently] seek Him." If you want a closer walk with the Lord, seek Him out. He is reaching out to you, but He is waiting for you to seek Him back.

The list of what Scripture says about who the Lord is to us could go on for pages: God is all-knowing, all-powerful, faithful, true, and so much more. Feel free to continue your own study of who God is as revealed by Scripture. But now, it is time to consider some people in the Bible to learn more about encountering God and who God is toward us.

David is the only man in Scripture called "A man after God's own heart." Does that mean God approved of all that David did? Not at all. As we mentioned earlier, David broke most of the ten commandments. He lived a life of great violence at times, told lies that resulted in men's deaths, acted on covetousness thoughts, the list goes on. No, God isn't saying these actions are good. Rather, He is showing that David's response to his circumstances and his own failings was to seek God's heart. He is showing that David's faith and heart in the psalms which David wrote are what make him a man after God's own heart.

David sought to be near God, no matter what was going on. The enemy was attacking—he went to God. He just won a victory—he went to God.

He'd just been confronted about his sin—he went to God. He believed what God said, he believed God would do what He said He would, and he praised God every step of the way.

We can also look at the life of Jesus. Repeatedly, Jesus goes away to pray. He goes to the mountains, the wilderness, or a secluded place. He went early in the morning or stayed there praying all through the night. He took time to pray and to commune with the Father.

John 5:19^C says, "Therefore Jesus answered and was saying to them, 'Truly, truly, I say to you, the Son can do nothing of Himself, unless it is something He sees the Father doing; for whatever the Father does, these things the Son also does in like manner.'" Jesus only did what He saw the Father doing and said what He heard the Father saying.

In John 14:9^B He says, "Whoever has seen me has seen the Father." Jesus healed the sick and ate with sinners. He rejected those who lived by religious traditions and laws that didn't touch their hearts. When the religious leaders encountered God in the flesh, they didn't recognize Him. They wanted to kill Him because He threatened what they felt comfortable with.

Each disciple encountered God in a way that took them from ordinary men to world changers. In their lifetime, the gospel spread from a small group in Judea throughout the Roman world. The apostle Paul died for a faith that he, at one point, tried to destroy. There are so many biographies of Christians throughout history who were transformed by knowing God. Each of us should have a similar story about how knowing God has changed us.

So, what about you?

1. Have you ever felt as though you were in the presence of God? What were the circumstances and how did it make you feel?

Encountering God

2. Did anyone ever tell you that chasing an experience or the presence of God would leave you disappointed and disillusioned? How has this affected your relationship with Him?

3. Have you ever wished God came to protect us from the world, rather than coming to send us out into the world? Why is understanding His goodness so important in our commission?

4. Have you ever really felt the love of God before? What were the circumstances? How did you react?

5. Do you believe that God is for you and not against you? Why or why not?

6. Have you tested God's promise that He rewards those who earnestly seek Him? If not, why not? If so, what happened?

7. What does it mean to you that God delights in you? How do you respond to that?

8. How has knowing God changed you?

CHAPTER 5

Incomplete Understanding

*As the heavens are higher than the earth,
so are my ways higher than your ways
and my thoughts than your thoughts.*

- Isaiah 55:9[A]

Having meditated on who God is and what His heart is toward you, we need to go back and address areas of tension in the Bible. In an academic and scientific society, education is revered, and intelligence is a key aspect of determining the worth of other people's words. In the circles I was influenced by, understanding Scripture and being able to rationally explain hard biblical topics were important. Without it, you were considered uneducated and had no chance of persuading others that what you believed was correct.

At the same time, there are so many areas of the Bible where even the wisest and most educated people disagree. Personally, I like things to fit neatly into little boxes. I like to have both my internal and external world organized. I have also always feared criticism of my ideas as being inaccurate.

There are many places in Scripture where seeming inconsistencies leave room for academics outside the church to point to. They claim these are examples of why the Bible isn't true and can't be trusted. Countless books have been written to disprove it.

I thought I needed to find a way to patch those holes with my own limited understanding in order to feel comfortable, organized, and correct. One of my biggest downfalls was needing everything to fit together perfectly in my mind.

Let's get really honest for a moment. It is all well and good to take our theologies and place them on a shelf while we dive into knowing God more. But, in an effort to know God more, we need to spend a lot of time with God and a lot of time in the Word. And when we spend much time in the Word of God, well, we run into problems, even with our theology on the shelf.

Examples such as the entire book of Job, the story of Elisha and the boys eaten by bears (2 Kings 2:23-25), God striking people down for touching the ark of the covenant when they tripped (2 Samuel 6:6-7), Ananias and Sapphira (Acts 5:1-10), Jesus cursing the fig tree (Mark 11:12-25), the 10th plague (Exodus 11-12), Lot offering his daughters (Genesis 19), not to mention a number of odd laws in Leviticus, and more.

All of these stories should cause a normal person to stop and question why they are even included in the Bible. It's hard to reconcile a loving God with the God portrayed in those stories from both the Old Testament and the New Testament. While there are ways to explain most of these—considering the culture, the language, the plan of God, the laws of sowing and reaping, human choice, and more—even with further understanding, these are still disconcerting.

Does that mean we should change the definition of unconditional love? Or does that mean we aren't clearly seeing those passages in the Old Testament? Unbelievers will say that we need to throw out the whole Bible. Some believers decide they will pick and choose.

I now land, along with some people I really respect, on the side with those who believe we don't change the core person and values of God as

Incomplete Understanding

revealed in Jesus simply based on stories like these in the Bible. But, we also don't throw out passages in the Bible that make us feel uncomfortable. We look at the original linguistic meaning, the cultural meaning, the prophetic meaning, and when we still don't understand, we don't change our foundational theology to make it fit.

Instead, we trust that one day we will know in full. We recognize that God's ways are so much higher than ours that we may never understand some Scriptures here on earth. And we take our questions and place them on a shelf, not swept under the bed, but just set aside to continue to consider as our faith grows. I realize now that explaining odd sounding stories in the Bible by changing foundational truths isn't doing us or anyone else any favors.

Romans 11:33[B] says, "Oh, the depth of the riches and wisdom and knowledge of God! How unsearchable are his judgments and how inscrutable his ways." We naturally want to make sense of God's judgments, but it is clear we cannot.

For example, when I look at the tenth plague discussed in Exodus 11-12, I can understand its context in the prophetic nature of the Passover, with Jesus being the Passover lamb and sacrifice in our place. I can also understand it in the context of being a consequence for the Egyptians who killed all the Israelite baby boys at the time of Moses' birth.

Yet even with those understandings, the idea of the Lord striking down all the firstborn, even of the animals, seems in stark contrast to John 10:10[D] that says, "The thief does not come except to steal, and to kill, and to destroy. I have come that they may have life, and that they may have it more abundantly."

If we believe God is the author of life and the enemy is the one who kills, steals, and destroys, then the language used in the passage in Exodus (and other parts of the Old Testament) can be confusing. I have heard some very good explanations about it, but nonetheless, the seeming contradiction remains in the text.

1 Corinthians 13:9-12^C says,

> *For we know in part and we prophesy in part; but when the perfect comes, the partial will be done away. When I was a child, I used to speak like a child, think like a child, reason like a child; when I became a man, I did away with childish things. For now we see in a mirror dimly, but then face to face; now I know in part, but then I will know fully just as I also have been fully known.*

I was never comfortable saying, except to people I deeply trusted, "I don't understand why the Bible says this. It is outside of who I understand God to be."

I still really want to reconcile and understand all of it. But, it seems like the Jewish religious leaders of Jesus' time missed recognizing who Jesus was because they tried to reconcile Scriptures and make them all fit a certain type of messiah and their traditional belief system. I'm realizing I also risk missing who Jesus is and what He is doing when my focus is instead on reconciling confusing Scriptures and seeking theological perfection.

The Old Testament is full of prophecies. Because the Pharisees had studied and decided that all the Scriptures about the coming of the Messiah needed to fit one time period, they tried to link them all together in a way that made sense. They didn't understand that the Messiah would come twice—once to save them by sacrificing Himself and then again as conquering King. Since Jesus didn't come as a conquering King the first time, they completely missed Him.

God purposely did not make it clear in the books of the prophets that the Messiah would come twice. God seems to like to hide Himself so that

Incomplete Understanding

we will search Him out. We must desire relationship before He begins to reveal the full picture. We see this in Jesus' ministry. Jesus even tells the disciples why in Matthew 13:10-17[A]:

The disciples came to him and asked, "Why do you speak to the people in parables?"

He replied, "Because the knowledge of the secrets of the kingdom of heaven has been given to you, but not to them. Whoever has will be given more, and they will have an abundance. Whoever does not have, even what they have will be taken from them. This is why I speak to them in parables:

Though seeing, they do not see;
 though hearing, they do not hear or understand.
In them is fulfilled the prophecy of Isaiah:

'You will be ever hearing but never understanding;
 you will be ever seeing but never perceiving.
For this people's heart has become calloused;
 they hardly hear with their ears,
 and they have closed their eyes.
Otherwise they might see with their eyes,
 hear with their ears,
 understand with their hearts
and turn, and I would heal them.'

But blessed are your eyes because they see, and your ears because they hear. For truly I tell you, many prophets and righteous people longed to see what you see but did not see it, and to hear what you hear but did not hear it."

Even that verse seems somewhat controversial. Jesus seems to be saying there is a secret knowledge that God has blinded certain people from seeing. But then Paul says the mystery has been revealed in Romans 16: 25b-26[1]:

> *This wonderful news includes the unveiling of the mystery kept secret from the dawn of creation until now. This mystery is understood through the prophecies of the Scripture and by the decree of the eternal God. And it is now heard openly by all the nations, igniting within them a deep commitment of faith.*

Here, Paul is saying that the secret of Scripture about the Messiah, which the Jews had not understood, is now revealed and available to people from all nations. Now, the revelation of the way to salvation is available to all who would believe in Jesus.

Outside of that, we go back to where Jesus says in Matthew 11:25[C], "At that time Jesus said, 'I praise You, Father, Lord of heaven and earth, that You have hidden these things from the wise and intelligent and have revealed them to infants.'" God seems to prefer that we come as children—that we let go of all our adult thinking and experiences and expectations just believe that anything is possible, like children do.

We should, of course, grow beyond spiritual milk to spiritual meat, but He seems to want us to maintain childlike faith. He hides from us so that we can find Him, not so that we miss Him. When you are in a relationship with someone, do you want them to put in effort to get to know you? Or do you lay everything out at the beginning for them, whether they seem interested or not? Most people wait to see how invested the other person is in the relationship before opening up completely.

How off-putting would it be if, when you first met someone, they let you know that they had researched you, stalked you online and know everything you've shared there, and did a background check on you? And then, they proceed to not listen to what you have to say since they think they already know everything about you?

Incomplete Understanding

It seems that's often what we do with God. But if we want to know God more, we need to press in more. We will still only know in part, but we will increasingly know God better.

In my old theology, my relationship with God was very task- and trial-oriented, because I believed God had chosen me for a relationship that I couldn't refuse and now my job was to obey His rules. I only knew a few ways to grow closer to God. I could grow closer by having a quiet time every day and doing good deeds, but if I stopped, I messed up that relationship. I could also grow closer by going through the trials He gave me with faith and thanksgiving. Any relationship progress was slow, and I could easily regress if I failed a task.

Now I see that I was living more like a slave than as a child of God and the bride of Christ. As in any relationship, it requires effort on both sides in order to increase intimacy. God's not a dictator, He's a loving partner. One who certainly knows more than us, so His advice and plans can be trusted. But He isn't forcing us to do anything. He wants us to feel loved, cherished, free, and powerful. We will talk more about our identity in Him in a later chapter.

I was so concerned that people respect my faith as logical, I forgot that faith sometimes just needs to be faith. How will I have faith to believe God for the miraculous if I don't have faith that He can reconcile His loving nature and the odd stories of His nature in the Old Testament?

In another interesting twist, Jesus teaches His disciples about faith in a way that brings up even more questions. In Mark 11:21-25[B] it says,

> *And Peter remembered and said to him, "Rabbi, look! The fig tree that you cursed has withered." And Jesus answered them, "Have faith in God. Truly, I say to you, whoever says to this mountain, 'Be taken up and thrown into the sea,' and does not doubt in his heart, but believes that what he says will come to pass, it will be done for*

> *him. Therefore I tell you, whatever you ask in prayer, believe that you have received it, and it will be yours."*

This is one of those stories that I mentioned earlier which is difficult to process. On one level, I don't understand why Jesus cursed the fig tree so that it died for not having fruit out of season. In our world, where people are concerned for our planet, even the life of trees seems to have value.

In the garden, Adam was told to care for the plants and animals. But we may get an idea of what Jesus is symbolically trying to say from 2 Timothy 4:2[A], "Preach the word; be prepared in season and out of season." Here we are called to be ready in season and out of season, and we know we are to bear good fruit.

But the bigger message Jesus is teaching the disciples is that if they had faith in God and did not doubt, then they had the power to speak and what they said would come to pass, just as Jesus spoke to the fig tree and what He said came to pass. On some level it is a warning as well as an encouragement. We don't get to dismiss the lesson because we aren't fully comfortable with the example. Literally, the power of life and death are in the tongue (Proverbs 18:21), and we haven't embraced the power within us that Jesus says is available.

Ultimately, we need to manage our hearts when there are unanswered questions. Once we have decided that these parts of Scripture that seem to disagree won't destroy our faith, and if we are willing to live with them in this tension, then we must be careful not to become double-minded. We need to continually remind ourselves of who God is, what He has promised us, and who we are in Christ so that we can stand firm on those truths.

When I finally took a step back and realized what I was doing by trying to force all the confusing parts of Scripture to fit into a theology, God showed me Ephesians 3:17b-19[A], and it changed me profoundly:

Incomplete Understanding

And I pray that you, being rooted and established in love, may have power, together with all the Lord's holy people, to grasp how wide and long and high and deep is the love of Christ, and to know this love that surpasses knowledge—that you may be filled to the measure of all the fullness of God.

Knowing the love of Christ actually surpasses knowledge. This may not be quite so profound for you, but it was to me. I thought I knew the love of God, but I didn't know the *love that surpasses knowledge*. Knowledge may lead you to God, but it will not change you.

The love of Christ is what transforms us. Without it, all we have is a full mind and maybe a puffed-up sense of pride. I, unconsciously, put knowledge before love. The result did not bring the fruit of the Spirit.

The more you try to make everything fit theologically without allowing for some tension, the less peace you have. It's like trying to work on several puzzles, all at the same time, without having all of the pieces yet, and while you only vaguely know what the finished puzzles will look like. And that is a simplified example!

But the peace of God surpasses those areas where we don't fully understand. If we let those places just be and focus on God, Philippians 4:7[B] says, "And the peace of God, which surpasses all understanding, will guard your hearts and your minds in Christ Jesus." The peace itself is something we cannot understand.

We want to fit a God who is outside of space, outside of time, outside of everything that is created into what our finite minds can comprehend. And we want to do it while still being able to process all the normal life stuff we need to use our mental capacity for. We try to do it by studying a book—a compilation of 66 books—which we somehow believe can reveal to us this limitless God and His magnificent plan in more than just the most basic of ways.

When you look at how intricately the human body was designed, how new life is formed in a mother's womb, how the whole earth is placed just perfectly on its axis, and turns at just the right speed, if you consider all that is in the universe, we realize it's silly to assume we can understand everything about God and why He does what He does. In Psalm 8:4-9^E David says,

> *When I look at the night sky and see the work of your fingers—*
>   *the moon and the stars you set in place—*
> *what are mere mortals that you should think about them,*
>   *human beings that you should care for them?*
> *Yet you made them only a little lower than God*
>   *and crowned them with glory and honor.*
> *You gave them charge of everything you made,*
>   *putting all things under their authority—*
> *the flocks and the herds*
>   *and all the wild animals,*
> *the birds in the sky, the fish in the sea,*
>   *and everything that swims the ocean currents.*
>
> *O Lord, our Lord, your majestic name fills the earth!*

It seems we are supposed to realize that God is so much greater and higher and amazing because he's beyond understanding. So, instead of trying to fit everything into our understanding, we should respond by honoring and glorifying God in worship for who He is. Now when we find ourselves in a place where we don't understand what God is saying, let's welcome His peace over that area, remember how great and awesome and beyond comprehension He is, and worship as David did.

It's not an easy place for me to be, agreeing that there are parts of the Scripture I don't understand, and choosing to be at peace with that. I remind myself that scripture doesn't say "have an answer for every criticism leveled against the Bible." Rather, it says in 1 Peter 3:15b-16^A:

Incomplete Understanding

"Always be prepared to give an answer to everyone who asks you to give the reason for the hope that you have. But do this with gentleness and respect..."

As you reflect on this chapter, take a moment to consider these questions. I would love to hear your answers:

1. What stories in the Bible do you struggle with?

2. How do you respond to the verse about how we only "know in part"?

3. How comfortable are you with areas of Scripture that seem contradictory? How do you manage your heart in those areas?

4. Do you struggle with being double minded? How do you reconcile it?

5. Perhaps you don't struggle with the issues raised in this chapter. If not, in what areas of your life and faith do you most try to protect yourself?

6. What did you think about the verse that talks about "Christ's love that surpasses knowledge"?

7. How often do you press in to know God more—to seek out mysteries He wants you to find?

8. What will you take away from this chapter?

CHAPTER 6

Tactics of the Enemy

You are of God, little children, and have overcome them, because He who is in you is greater than he who is in the world.

- 1 John 4:4^D

I'd much rather focus on how awesome God is and how much more powerful He is than to focus on the enemy. And since we have the same power that raised Christ from the dead living in us, we are more powerful than the enemy when we walk in God's power. But, understanding some of the enemy's tactics can help us recognize and avoid the snares he sets for us. So, let's shine our light on some of the methods the devil uses so we can learn to avoid falling into his traps.

1. Questioning and twisting God's Word

Questioning the Word of God is an interesting balance, because we should analyze the Word and consider our understanding of it in an effort to grow closer to God. Asking questions about why God said this, or how a certain passage fits in can help us learn and grow.

But when it's the enemy questioning the Word of God, usually it's to draw us into sin, separate us from God, and twist the meaning of what the Word of God actually says. It brings bad fruit instead of good.

It's a tactic the enemy uses time and again. You could say it's literally the oldest trick in the book. Let's take a look back at the beginning in Genesis 3:1-5[B].

> *Now the serpent was more crafty than any other beast of the field that the Lord God had made.*
>
> *He said to the woman, "Did God actually say, 'You shall not eat of any tree in the garden'?" And the woman said to the serpent, "We may eat of the fruit of the trees in the garden, but God said, 'You shall not eat of the fruit of the tree that is in the midst of the garden, neither shall you touch it, lest you die.'" But the serpent said to the woman, "You will not surely die. For God knows that when you eat of it your eyes will be opened, and you will be like God, knowing good and evil."*

Here, the serpent both questions and misquotes what God said in order to make Eve question what she heard. Then the serpent contradicts what God said, introducing doubt, and plants his own seed in her mind that God might not have her best interests at heart and might be keeping something good from her. She falls for it.

Jump forward approximately four thousand years and the devil tries to do the same thing with Jesus. Yes, he attempts to twist God's word while speaking to *the Word* (Jesus). Matthew 4:5-7[D] says,

> *Then the devil took Him up into the holy city, set Him on the pinnacle of the temple, and said to Him, "If You are the Son of God, throw Yourself down. For it is written:*
>
> > *'He shall give His angels charge over you,'*
>
> *and,*
> > *'In their hands they shall bear you up,*
> > *Lest you dash your foot against a stone.'"*

> *Jesus said to him, "It is written again, 'You shall not tempt the Lord your God.'"*

The devil is quoting Psalm 91:11-12. The quote may be direct, but the heart of this Scripture is not to test God, but to believe God is faithful. The devil is twisting it for his own purposes. And how does Jesus respond? He responds with another Scripture.

Let us fill our hearts and minds with God's Word, not to puff ourselves up, but to secure our belt of truth that holds our weapons to use against the enemy and keeps our armor secured. We can refute the enemy's attempt to twist and question Scripture the same way Jesus did—with solid truth.

2. Questioning our identity

In that same passage from Matthew, the devil says, "If you are the Son of God…" How often do we recoil when someone questions our identity, authority, position, or place? But you will notice, Jesus doesn't even address this jab. He is confident in who He is.

Being secure in our identity is crucial if we're to stand firm against the enemy and to step into the calling God placed on our life. For this reason, we are going to spend the next chapter looking at what our God-given identity is. Do not forget who you are in Him.

3. Making us think he is more powerful so that we fear him

As I began writing this chapter, I started to feel anxious. I know this information is something the enemy would love to have me skip or mess up. All these fears started buzzing in my mind. But I know the greatest victories are on the other side of fear. 2 Timothy 1:7[E] says, "For God has not given us a spirit of fear and timidity, but of power, love, and self-discipline."

The enemy only has the power over us that we give him. James 4:7[B] says, "Submit yourselves therefore to God. Resist the devil, and he will flee from you." This verse says the enemy will actually flee from you when you are submitting to God and resisting the devil.

The enemy has been defeated by what Jesus did in His death and resurrection. He is on borrowed time, and he knows it, but he doesn't want us to know it. 1 John 5:18b-19[A] says, "the One who was born of God keeps them safe, and the evil one cannot harm them. We know that we are children of God, and that the whole world is under the control of the evil one."

Also, Luke 10:17-20[D] says,

> *Then the seventy returned with joy, saying, "Lord, even the demons are subject to us in Your name."*
>
> *And He said to them, "I saw Satan fall like lightning from heaven. Behold, I give you the authority to trample on serpents and scorpions, and over all the power of the enemy, and nothing shall by any means hurt you. Nevertheless do not rejoice in this, that the spirits are subject to you, but rather rejoice because your names are written in heaven."*

This is so definitive about the authority we have, but this authority is not our focus. We should be much more focused on what we have been given in our eternal salvation. Our authority over the enemy is so minor in the grand scheme of things that it is not even worth comparing to the rest of our inheritance. And yet, it is still part of our inheritance—a part that may Christians have completely overlooked or forgotten about. We have authority over *all* the power of the enemy.

4. Putting thoughts in our mind and making us think they are our own

And even worse than just putting thoughts in our mind, he then follows it up with thoughts in our mind that judge ourselves for thinking those thoughts!

I've known for years that I am called to take my thoughts captive and make them obedient to God (2 Corinthians 10:5). I began learning how to do that more than ten years ago. At the time, I knew the enemy could attack my thoughts, and I began seeing negative thoughts about myself as the lies they really were.

Those thoughts were in opposition to what the Bible said, such as, "I am not valuable," and "I don't have anything to offer," as well as many others I can't even remember, because they have long since lost power over me. Being able to say, "This thought is a lie," and then taking it captive and speaking truth over it, has been life changing.

Even knowing that, it wasn't until the past year, as I learned more about how to recognize God's voice, that I've realized how many random thoughts pop into my head that aren't mine. I always thought they were mine because they sounded the same in my head as all my other thoughts.

Sure, plenty of them are mine, but many are not. Some are God speaking to me—usually these thoughts are kinder and nicer than my own, either toward me or others. Sometimes it's random thoughts about other people who, I now realize, God wants me to intercede for or reach out to. It has been so amazing to start recognizing God's voice. (We will talk more about learning to recognize God's voice in an upcoming chapter.)

But as I've learned to consider the thoughts in my head in order to recognize when God is speaking, I've also started to notice all these other random thoughts that are not God speaking and are not my own. Sometimes they are so obvious they are funny. Other times they are so horrible that I'm glad no one can hear my thoughts.

When I believed these were my thoughts, before I learned to discern my voice and God's voice and the enemy's voice, I would feel so unclean, awful, or even depraved. I wanted to get away from those thoughts as quickly as possible. Knowing now that the thought isn't mine, I just push it aside and happily move on to the good things God is saying.

Just so you can start considering how this works in your own head, I'll give two examples, one that I recognized immediately and one that took me years to see as the voice of the enemy.

One day, while out in my neighborhood, I noticed a car running in a neighbor's driveway and no one was around. The thought popped into my head, "I could steal that car right now." If I were a different type of person, or if I was in a different circumstance in life, perhaps the thought wouldn't have been so farfetched. But, you see, I'm a rule follower.

I never want to ask anyone to make exceptions for me for any rule, no matter how small. The idea of breaking a law makes my heart pound in a panicked way. I also hate driving. I don't like driving the car that my husband and I own. I don't even like riding in cars. Clearly, this is a ridiculous thought for me.

I had no problem setting that thought aside and laughing! You may still think the thought was mine, but I knew the moment it popped up that it sounded nothing like me. Most of the time the enemy is more subtle, but sometimes I think he just wants to see how far he can push it. A more likely thought, if it were mine, would have been something like, "Someone could steal that car. I should watch to make sure no one steals it."

The other example I'm going to share is one that is much more serious in nature. On the Sunday in church where God really drove this point home to me, our pastor was speaking on this topic. I'd already had the aforementioned experience and was already identifying thoughts of the enemy. But something the pastor said made me remember a very dark time in my life, a time when I thought I was suicidal.

It was many years ago, before I understood how to take thoughts captive and how to recognize when the enemy is speaking. It is a time in my life that very few people know about because I felt deep shame about it. I suddenly saw that whole time in my life reframed, finally understanding that the enemy was invading my mind. The reason it finally clicked was because the pastor said that the way to recognize the thoughts of the enemy is that his thoughts are not in line with our *other* thoughts.

It immediately became clear that those suicidal thoughts from all those years ago contrasted with my other thoughts at the time. I wanted to live. I was afraid of those thoughts. I was afraid of what I believed those thoughts might make me do.

[I will interject that I do not believe that all or even most depressed and suicidal people are experiencing what I was, but certainly some may be. If you feel like you do not want to live or are thinking about harming yourself in any way, please reach out to someone; there are so many resources available to help. Call the National Suicide Prevention Lifeline at 1-800-273-8255 if you need support.]

I hope your experiences with the enemy were not that extreme, but when we know how to recognize his thoughts in our mind, we can much more easily say, "that's not mine" and ask God to speak a better word to us.

5. Giving us a spirit of fear

Fear, anxiety, and worry are never from the Lord, yet so many believers find themselves consumed by these feelings. The enemy likes to disguise fearful thoughts as wisdom. For instance, we believe: *this thing I'm afraid of is dangerous or harmful, so I am being smart when I agree with these anxious thoughts and continue to replay them in my mind.* But that is not what God says.

Philippians 4:6-7[A] says, "Do not be anxious about anything, but in every situation, by prayer and petition, with thanksgiving, present your requests to God. And the peace of God, which transcends all understanding, will guard your hearts and your minds in Christ Jesus." It also says, in 2 Timothy 1:7[D], "For God has not given us a spirit of fear, but of power and of love and of a sound mind."

Just as we must take captive our fearful thoughts, we should also take captive our fearful emotions. One of the best ways I've personally found to dispel fear is to begin to worship or listen to worship music. It is often the last thing I want to do, but once I begin, the feeling of fear begins to dispel. Worshiping the Prince of Peace brings peace to my heart and mind.

Another way to combat fear is to tell another believer that you are battling anxiety. Just inviting someone else into the battle to pray for and encourage you can be helpful.

For those who are battling mental illness, while I firmly believe God can and does heal mental illness, please seek help from a professional until you are completely free. Christians who are physically sick still see doctors. Christians battling mental illness should be no different.

6. Coming when we are weak and appealing to our human needs and desires

As humans, we have basic needs such as water, food, air, sleep, and shelter. We have higher needs as well, but these basic needs must be met first. The enemy's first attempt to tempt Jesus was with a basic need.

Luke 4:1-3[B] says,

> *And Jesus, full of the Holy Spirit, returned from the Jordan and was led by the Spirit in the wilderness for forty days, being tempted by the devil. And he ate nothing during those days. And when they were ended, he was hungry. The devil said to him, "If you are the Son of God, command this stone to become bread."*

Jesus clearly had a physical need. We see later in Jesus' ministry that He does multiple miracles to provide food for people. We see in the Old Testament where God provided both food and water supernaturally for people. What was wrong with Jesus just giving in and making bread?

Jesus was both fully human and fully God. The enemy knew Jesus could turn the stone into bread. It would not have been a temptation if He wasn't able to do it. But Jesus was fully human so that He could connect with us and understand what we experience, like hunger, and so His sacrifice as a perfect human could atone for our sins.

Hebrews 4:15[C] says, "For we do not have a high priest who cannot sympathize with our weaknesses, but One who has been tempted in all things as we are, yet without sin."

The enemy knows we are at our weakest when we are hungry, tired, fearful, lonely, and desperate. We should also recognize these moments for what they are and be aware that the thoughts and attitudes we have at these times are often temptations by the enemy.

In my house, the time right before dinner tends to be crisis time. We all have problems when we get "hangry." With five of us in the house, somehow at least one person is having a meltdown during this time of day.

Once we realized the problem wasn't us, but legitimate needs crying out to be met and the enemy taking advantage of those unmet needs, we changed a few things. We let everyone eat healthy snacks, even if they don't eat as much dinner. We try to make dinner time earlier. We try to give more grace in that time. Do we still have problems? Yes. Has it improved? Definitely.

Another example is that I try to avoid having important conversations with my husband when we are hungry or tired. When our basic needs are met, it is much easier to be compassionate, understanding, patient, and kind to one another.

Recognizing that your thoughts and attitudes are more susceptible to the enemy at these times should help you develop strategies to stand against him.

7. Tempting us with a shortcut

The third method the enemy used against Jesus was tempting Him to skip the hard stuff. Matthew 4:8-10^G says,

> *Again, the devil took Him up on a very high mountain and showed Him all the kingdoms of the world and the glory [splendor, magnificence, and excellence] of them; and he said to Him, "All these things I will give You, if You fall down and worship me." Then Jesus said to him, "Go away, Satan! For it is written and forever remains written, 'You shall worship the Lord your God, and serve Him only.'"*

The enemy thought he knew from Scripture what Jesus' final goal was, reigning over the kingdoms of the world in glory. Zechariah 14:9^C says, "And the Lord will be king over all the earth; in that day the Lord will be the only one, and His name the only one."

Jesus came to save the world and set us free and He will one day reign as king. The devil was offering Jesus a shortcut to the end goal, one that would give the enemy what he wanted as well. The offer is to skip the hard part of conquering, and, unbeknownst to the devil, skip the cross. But in return, the devil wants Jesus to bow to him.

There are so many times in life where we wish we could take a shortcut or an easy way out. In those times, the devil likes to offer us shortcuts. But the shortcut only gets you to the end, it doesn't accomplish all that needs to happen along the way. If Jesus skipped the cross, He would have missed His real purpose of saving us.

While God is not the author of bad things, we can still give Him glory when we walk through hard seasons. God doesn't waste the difficult times. Instead, He uses them for our benefit. And, when we look back from the end, we see how the shortcut would have short-changed us.

Instead of being tempted to take a path you know is not from God, worship and praise Him in the hard times. Refuse to take a different way other than God's way, knowing that God won't waste it and what the enemy intended for evil, God will turn to good for you.

We position ourselves powerfully in the unseen spiritual battles when we worship in difficult seasons. We ensure victory when we stay on God's path.

8. Taking something good to an extreme

It's very likely that the original intentions behind the Pharisees were good. The nation of Israel had fallen so many times into a cycle of disobedience and punishment, they knew they needed to work harder at not falling away from the law of God. So, they set up all these extra rules to try to keep themselves from even coming close to breaking the actual rules.

Along the way, their hearts moved away from God. They eventually cared more about how well they followed all the rules and the honor and prestige of their position than the people they should have been serving.

Paul is constantly reminding the churches not to go to extremes. A good chunk of Romans is Paul bringing up arguments from one side or another, trying to get the believers back to the truth in the middle. An example is in Romans 5 and 6. At the end of chapter 5, he is talking about grace, so in Romans 6:1-2^B, he feels he needs to say, "What shall we say then? Are we to continue in sin that grace may abound? By no means! How can we who died to sin still live in it?"

The enemy likes to show us something true, like grace, and then push us further until we say, well, sin doesn't matter, I'm under grace.

In our society today, it seems that people want to take all their beliefs and passions to the extreme. When someone takes an extreme position that is in opposition to your view, even if you feel only moderately passionate about your belief, you may feel that you have to argue a more extreme version of your position to balance out the conversation.

Their extreme invites you to be more extreme. Instead of falling into this, avoid conflict for the sake of unity when possible. Engage only with gentleness and love, and only when the other person's goal is also a dialogue.

9. Making us confident in areas of error and questioning in areas of truth

The enemy loves to encourage you to solidify any deception he's helped you fall for until you are confident and proud of it—like taking pride in all you do for God. Or taking pride in how zealous you are against sinners. Or taking pride in how moral you are compared to others. Like I mentioned before, looking for areas of pride can reveal possible areas of incorrect thinking when we realize how the devil likes to use it to cover up his work.

While he likes to make you confident in your incorrect thinking, he also likes to make you feel uncertain about actual truths. Does God really love you? How could He love a sinner like you? Is God really for you? Look at all these bad things in your life. Would a God who is for you let that happen? Are you really saved? You haven't even talked to God this week? Don't listen to his lies. If you are tempted to believe any of these, be sure to read on in the next chapter where we talk about our identity in Christ.

10. Encouraging overthinking

This is a big way he gets to me. I'll have a thought or feeling, after the fact, about something that happened, something someone said, or something I said. All of a sudden, I'll have a thought that someone interpreted something wrong. Or I'll suddenly wonder if they meant something else.

Worse, I'll have the thought that they must be upset with me, even if I didn't think so at the time. This will cause my emotions to change. From there, I'll just replay the scene over and over in my head until it becomes something completely different than it was in the moment. In the past, I wouldn't really notice or stop myself when I was getting sucked in.

Now, I see it starting and I will try to break out. Most of the time, I must repeatedly partner with God as it continues to come to mind and I don't want to go there. Sometimes I'll even just check in with a person to get it to go away: "Did you mean this? Did you think I meant that?" It's pretty much never what my overthinking believes it was.

On the flip side, if we ever do accidentally offend someone, the devil has no reason to bring it up over and over in our mind so we can make it right. He'd be happy for us to be ignorant forever of the offence.

11. Dismissing nudges from the Holy Spirit

The enemy likes to distract us from hearing God. A still, small nudge from God can often be disregarded. Perhaps you get a thought that you are overlooking something in Scripture. Or perhaps you feel you should probably stop doing something that isn't entirely sinful, but you think God might be telling you to stop. Perhaps you feel you should go talk to someone or encourage someone, but you don't know why.

We can feel somewhat unsettled by these stirrings if we haven't been engaging with them regularly. It isn't comfortable to think you could be wrong about a Scripture, or to give up something you enjoy, or to approach someone you haven't spoken to in a while. The enemy likes to encourage your discomfort and lead you to dismiss these as nothing more than some weird feelings not in any way connected to God.

12. Leading us to prioritize less important doctrines

This one should sound familiar to you. Since we have covered this in great depth in previous chapters, we won't spend much time here. We saw the example of how believing God cares more about morality than love affected the rest of my understanding of God. (I never would have said that, but, looking back, it is how I stacked my beliefs.) This is an effective way to derail people by giving them a false view of God. We need to look to what Jesus prioritized in His ministry.

This tactic is one that also leads to disunity in the church, and it can even lead to churches splitting. Certainly, it can be hard to be in the same church when you have two different ideas about how a church should be run, but Jesus was passionate about the unity of the Church—the whole body of Christ. On the day of His death, unity was the main message and prayer He had for His disciples.

13. Making us believe he is fictional

I had a religion professor in college who seemed to not believe that the devil was real and active. He's not the only Christian I've encountered who thinks the devil is merely allegorical. While we just saw that the enemy has been defeated, 1 Peter 5:8-9[A] says,

> *Be alert and of sober mind. Your enemy the devil prowls around like a roaring lion looking for someone to devour. Resist him, standing firm in the faith, because you know that the family of believers throughout the world is undergoing the same kind of suffering*

While we should not be afraid of the enemy because, in Christ, we have power over him, we should also not overlook the fact that he is seeking to devour any who are unprepared. If we don't know we have an enemy, then we won't understand all these previous deceptions.

Beyond watching for these tactics just discussed, we have many verses in Scripture that encourage us and tell us how to have victory over the enemy. So, here are ways we can actively engage against the enemy.

Put on the armor of God

Whether we believe it or not, we live in the midst of a spiritual battle. The war may have already been won, but the enemy is going to take out as many as he can before the final judgement. We cannot be passive in the battle. Ephesians 6:10-12[B] says,

> *Finally, be strong in the Lord and in the strength of his might. Put on the whole armor of God, that you may be able to stand against the schemes of the devil. For we do not wrestle against flesh and blood, but against the rulers, against the authorities, against the*

cosmic powers over this present darkness, against the spiritual forces of evil in the heavenly places.

There is an unseen battle that you've been given special armor for. There are plenty of books that unpack each part of our spiritual armor mentioned in scripture. Make sure you know what you have and wear it properly.

Resist the enemy and don't give him a foothold

Resisting is not a passive action. Resistance is something you must actively engage in. As the verse in 1 Peter mentioned, the devil is on the prowl, looking for those he might devour.

Ephesians 4:27[C] says, "and do not give the devil an opportunity." You open and close doors in your life that the enemy can access. Choose to keep them closed.

Forgive others

Unforgiveness is one of those footholds the devil likes to take. Ephesians 4:25-27[A] says, "Therefore each of you must put off falsehood and speak truthfully to your neighbor, for we are all members of one body. 'In your anger do not sin': Do not let the sun go down while you are still angry, and do not give the devil a foothold."

Also, 2 Corinthians 2:10-11[E] says, "When you forgive this man, I forgive him, too. And when I forgive whatever needs to be forgiven, I do so with Christ's authority for your benefit, so that Satan will not outsmart us. For we are familiar with his evil schemes." The enemy tries to get us to hold on to unforgiveness, but when we are aware of his schemes, as Paul says, he cannot outsmart us.

Trust in the finished work of Jesus and our heritage

1 John 3:8b[B] says, "The reason the Son of God appeared was to destroy the works of the devil." Jesus came and completed the work He was sent to do, conquering sin and death and opening the way to eternal Life. Isaiah 54:17[A] says, "'no weapon forged against you will prevail, and you will refute every tongue that accuses you. This is the heritage of the servants of the Lord, and this is their vindication from me,' declares the Lord."

The enemy may try to condemn you and raise his voice against you in accusation, but it will not succeed. We have assurance of victory. Romans 16:20a[C] says, "The God of peace will soon crush Satan under your feet." We don't have to wonder about or doubt the outcome, we just need to stand firm in the promises of God.

Be confident in your identity in Christ

Knowing who you are in Christ is crucial to not being deceived by the enemy. If you know who you are, you can recognize when the enemy starts whispering lies to you. This topic really needs its own chapter, so we will cover it in detail next.

First, let's reflect on this chapter.

1. Do you recognize the enemy using any of these tactics against you? In what areas of your life?

2. How often do you see him using these tactics on people around you? What do you do with that information?

3. In what areas can you make strides to avoid the schemes of the devil? What practical things can you do?

4. What area of your life has been most battered by the enemy? Is there a reason that area has been his focus?

5. Which of the methods to victory do you need to be more active in?

CHAPTER 7

Our Identity

*For you created my inmost being;
you knit me together in my mother's womb.
I praise you because I am fearfully and wonderfully made;
your works are wonderful,
I know that full well.*

Psalm 139:13-14[A]

You need to know that, as a Christian, you have an identity that is completely unrelated to what you do and the past you've come from. If you thought, like me, that your Christian identity depended on how well you've done on God's moral scale or how much you have served in the church or community, you've missed it.

Does this give us license to sin? No. Does this mean we don't need to have good works? No. It means you have value and an identity before you've done any of it. And that if you rest in your God-given identity, those things will be natural fruit.

I didn't understand that knowing who God is and knowing who I am is crucial to bearing good fruit. As an analogy, He showed me an image of a plant trying to grow a rose with no success. But the plant isn't a rose bush. It's a cherry tree.

When you try to produce what you think you should when you don't know who you are created to be, all the effort and hard work won't produce anything good. But when you understand you should be creating cherry blossoms and cherries, and you realize you're rooted in God, who wants to use you, and you let Him fill you with the nutrients you need, you will produce blossoms and fruit with little effort on your own.

God was showing me that I was trying to be a rose bush, when I'm made to be a cherry tree. The relief I feel knowing I'm not intended to be a rose bush is enormous. I am free to be who God created me to be and my heart rejoices in that knowledge. Discover who God created you to be, and then you'll know what kind of fruit you should produce. You may be a blueberry bush, a pear tree, or a watermelon vine. If so, don't try to produce a rose or a cherry.

This is probably the chapter I need to read the most. Even though I had my theology messed up about God, I knew and could tell you what the Bible said about Him, and I thought I believed it. But my identity in Christ is something that I've been slower to learn and really believe. That is the correct order, though. We can't understand who we are in Christ before we understand who God is. And whenever my understanding about who God is changes, my understanding of who I am in Him will change as well.

I was talking with some friends the other day about ways to remind ourselves of who God is and who we are and the promises of Scripture. I was sharing with them that I have two playlists of worship songs, one with songs that really emphasize who God is and the other with songs that really emphasize who we are in Christ. One friend mentioned that she writes reminders of her identity on Post-It notes displayed around her house, and when she passes by one, she repeats it out loud to herself.

The first place to look for our identity in Christ is in what the Bible says about us. There are so many verses that I can't possibly cover them all, but I'm going to try to include as many as I can. Some of these apply to all people, but most only apply to those who have confessed Jesus as Lord and Savior.

We are CREATED IN GOD'S IMAGE

You are not merely dirt and dust. You are not an evolved monkey. You have special value because you are created in the image of God. Genesis 1:27[C] says, "God created man in His own image, in the image of God He created him; male and female He created them." This concept is of such importance that it is repeated twice in the same verse.

In both Genesis 9:6 and James 3:9, God tells us how we should relate to other people because people are made in the image of God. If you ever wonder if you have value, this is the place to start. You have value because you are created in God's image. This applies to all people, whether they believe or not.

We are LOVED BY GOD

I know we already covered that God is love in chapter five, but this is so incredibly important to understand that we're going to look again. This also applies to all people, saved or not.

Colossians 3:12a[H] says, "You are the people of God; He loved you and chose you for His own." We've already talked about John 3:16 and Romans 5:8, which are well known verses describing how loved we are by God. So, let's look at just how powerful the love of God is for us in Romans 8:35-39[B]. It says,

> *Who shall separate us from the love of Christ? Shall tribulation, or distress, or persecution, or famine, or nakedness, or danger, or sword? ... No, in all these things we are more than conquerors through him who loved us. For I am sure that neither death nor life, nor angels nor rulers, nor things present nor things to come, nor powers, nor height nor depth, nor anything else in all creation, will be able to separate us from the love of God in Christ Jesus our Lord.*

God's love for you is so powerful that nothing in all creation can separate you from it. There is no power great enough to make God stop loving you. No matter what you've done, no matter where you go, you are loved with an everlasting love (Jeremiah 31:3).

This needs to reach the deepest part of us to change us. When it becomes a core part of our identity, we won't be so concerned with what others think about us or what others can offer us. We will be more confident in stepping out and giving love to others.

We are SAVED

Obviously, this is only those people who have put their faith in God. Acts 2:21[C] says, "And it shall be that everyone who calls on the name of the Lord will be saved." And Romans 10:9[D] says, "If you confess with your mouth the Lord Jesus and believe in your heart that God has raised Him from the dead, you will be saved."

When you have confessed and believed, you can be assured of your salvation. As a result, we should live differently. Are you living as though you have been saved from death to life? Let's embrace our salvation.

We are FORGIVEN

As a result of Jesus' death on the cross, we have access to forgiveness. Acts 10:43[G] says, "All the prophets testify about Him, that through His name everyone who believes in Him [whoever trusts in and relies on Him, accepting Him as Savior and Messiah] receives forgiveness of sins." So, if you believe in Jesus as your Savior, your sins are forgiven.

Also, 1 John 2:12[A] says, "I am writing to you, dear children, because your sins have been forgiven on account of his name." Why then do we let ourselves be weighed down by our past? Let's claim our identity as forgiven and let it propel us to forgive others and live without the shame the enemy wants us to carry!

We are FREE

Not only are you forgiven, but you have been set free! Galatians 5:13[C] says, "For you were called to freedom, brethren; only do not turn your freedom into an opportunity for the flesh, but through love serve one another." Whether you feel free or not, if you believe in Jesus, He broke your chains of slavery to sin.

I don't think that I had ever really understood or accepted this freedom. I may have been free, but I still often lived like I was in bondage. Not to a specific sin, necessarily, just constantly beaten down by life and always reacting rather than being prepared. I was a slave to my flesh rather than free to walk in the fruit of the Spirit. I secretly felt like I was failing instead of feeling free to succeed. You see, you can be free but still live like you are not.

In the next chapter we will look at the Helper we've been given to help us walk in the freedom we already have access to.

We are HEALED

God did not save us and set us free so that we could still live broken lives, in sickness and despair. 1 Peter 2:24[B] says, "He himself bore our sins in his body on the tree, that we might die to sin and live to righteousness. By his wounds you have been *healed*." The word that is translated *healed* here is the Greek word *iathēte*. The word can be used for both spiritual and physical healing, but all forms of this verb are most often used to refer to physical healing. This verb is used in other places such as when

Jesus healed the paralytic and when the woman with the bleeding disorder touched His robe and was healed.

The passage in 1 Peter goes on to talk about how we are like sheep who have now returned to the care of the shepherd. God cares for us. He wants to see us well cared for, healthy and whole.

This concept was foreign to me before. I'm still processing all that it means. We will look more in depth at this concept in a later chapter.

We are a NEW CREATION

Who you were before has no bearing on who you are now. You are completely new. Nothing that had a hold on you before can have the same kind of hold on you now, unless you give it that power.

2 Corinthians 5:17[D] says, "Therefore, if anyone is in Christ, he is a new creation; old things have passed away; behold, all things have become new." None of your past has a say over who you are in Christ. Let's walk in our new life!

We are DELIVERED

We have been delivered from our enemy, from the kingdom of the world, and from the kingdom of darkness. Colossians 1:13-14[D] says "He has delivered us from the power of darkness and conveyed us into the kingdom of the Son of His love, in whom we have redemption through His blood, the forgiveness of sins."

The enemy no longer has power over us. He may try, but we have been delivered into the kingdom of Jesus, where our enemy has no power except what we give to him. So, stand firm in your identity and do not give the enemy power over you.

We are CONQUERORS

Not only are we delivered, we have become conquerors. Now we have nothing that can separate us from the love of God. We are no longer under condemnation but can now stand firm in victory. Romans 8:37[A] says, "No, in all these things we are more than conquerors through him who loved us."

The context of this verse is a chapter about how powerful God's love is, that nothing in all creation can separate us from God and His unfailing love for us. And here Paul specifically shows us that, as a result, we can stand powerfully and be victorious. When we doubt God's love, it can really affect our ability to be conquerors. But if we cling to the truth of God's love and remember our identity as conquerors, no one can stand against us.

We are BLESSED

There are so many places that talk about our blessings. Paul says in Ephesians 1:3[C], "Blessed be the God and Father of our Lord Jesus Christ, who has blessed us with every spiritual blessing in the heavenly places in Christ." And then in Philippians 4:19[G] it says, "And my God will liberally supply (fill until full) your every need according to His riches in glory in Christ Jesus." God's storehouse of blessings will never run out.

Do you trust that God wants to meet your needs? I've heard many stories from people about how God provided for them when they were in need, and not just those in desperate circumstances. We have certainly seen God's blessing in our lives, but perhaps not quite to the same extent.

It seems to happen far more often for people who expect God to bless them. I was always more expectant of a trial than a blessing in the past. I'm beginning to change that expectation to look for blessings.

We are ADOPTED

Do you feel at times as though you don't belong? Romans 8:15[A] says, "The Spirit you received does not make you slaves, so that you live in fear again; rather, the Spirit you received brought about your adoption to sonship. And by him we cry, 'Abba, Father.'"

You have a place. You have a Father. Whatever your earthly father was like, you have a perfect heavenly Father who would like to show you the absolute best a father can be. You are adopted into a loving family with a father who is rich beyond what you can imagine. Have you accepted your new status as God's child? Do you live like an orphan or like a son or daughter?

We are HEIRS

Being adopted also brings us another part of our identity. Romans 8:17[D] says, "and if children, then heirs—heirs of God and joint heirs with Christ, if indeed we suffer with Him, that we may also be glorified together." We are heirs of God.

We have an inheritance as 1 Peter 1:4[C] describes, "an inheritance which is imperishable and undefiled and will not fade away, reserved in heaven for you." You don't do anything to receive an inheritance. It simply comes to you.

We are THE LIGHT

Matthew 5:14[B] says, "You are the light of the world. A city set on a hill cannot be hidden." In our new identity, we have been called to shine for the world to see. We should draw the world to us and stand out, not hiding, but lighting the way to salvation.

There are far more pieces of our identity than I've covered here, but look at what an amazing identity we have in just what is listed above! I've known most of these verses for years, and yet I didn't live like I believed many of them.

I need to continually remind myself of who I am. Maybe you do, too. Perhaps, like my friend, you need to write a couple of those on post-it notes to place around your house and speak them out loud every time you pass them. Or maybe you have another way of reminding yourself of God's Word.

Being confident in these parts of our identity allows us to be open to the specific call of God on our own life. God has called and gifted you in specific ways. 1 Corinthians 12:17-19[A] says,

> *If the whole body were an eye, where would the sense of hearing be? If the whole body were an ear, where would the sense of smell be? But in fact God has placed the parts in the body, every one of them, just as he wanted them to be. If they were all one part, where would the body be?*

To understand who God has specifically created you to be, you need to be able to recognize what He is saying to you about the destiny He has for you.

Perhaps you are like I was, and the word *destiny* rubs you the wrong way. Maybe you, like me, don't feel like you have a destiny other than living a moral life, following Jesus, and doing the best you can in your family life and job. Maybe, like me, you took many spiritual gifts tests over the years and you felt discouraged every time you saw the results. Maybe you told yourself, "Well, I guess I'm just a less important part of the body." I'm about 20 years into my walk with God, and I am only now realizing I had a calling and destiny all along. I had spiritual gifts. I just didn't know how to access them.

Even after this realization, I still wasn't sure what my calling and destiny might be. At first, I thought maybe God just called me to be a mom. And He certainly did call me to be a mom. Do you know how I know that? I have children. So, I am called to be the best mom possible to those kids. And for a season of my life, I was called to make that pretty much my main focus. But that was not my main destiny. I couldn't understand why God hadn't told me, or told someone else to tell me what it was.

It took more than a year for me to begin to be able to hear what God was saying and see what He was doing in order to understand even part of where my calling might take me. You see, God is calling you to be a partner with Him, not simply a servant to Him.

1 Corinthians 3:8-9[D] says, "Now he who plants and he who waters are one, and each one will receive his own reward according to his own labor. For we are God's fellow workers; you are God's field, you are God's building."

It may take some time, but press in. It's worth every fumbled step to get to the place of hearing God's heart for you. For now, take a moment to reflect on these questions.

1. What kind of fruit have you been trying to produce? What kind of fruit are you created to produce?

2. Which of these aspects of your identity stood out the most to you? Why?

3. Which of these is the hardest for you to accept as true? Why do you think that is?

4. Which one of these is the identity you most needed to hear?

5. Which one of these identities is the easiest for you to accept?

6. How do you remind yourself of your identity in Christ?

7. Which one of these identities do you most need to remember about other people around you?

8. Have you ever felt God was calling you to something specific?

CHAPTER 8

The Holy Spirit

I will ask the Father, and He will give you another
Helper, that He may be with you forever.

- John 14:16[C]

Let's talk about the Holy Spirit.

How did you feel when you read that sentence? Did you get a sense of dread thinking this might be where the book gets too *out there* for you? Or did you feel bored, thinking you know all about the Holy Spirit? Or did you get excited when you read that? Like *finally, she's getting to the good stuff!* I'd love to know what your thoughts are right now, and then see if your expectations were correct when you've finished the chapter.

For me, I've always known about the Holy Spirit. It is hard to grow up in the church and not know that the third person of the Trinity is important. But somehow, in the churches I've been around and in my own walk, the Holy Spirit was always secondary to Jesus.

Jesus is our savior and our redeemer. We pray in Jesus' name and talk about the power in the blood of Jesus. We celebrate His life and resurrection. In a certain sense, talking about Jesus is safe. He came, lived a perfect life, died for our sins, and then ascended back up into heaven where He sits at the right hand of the Father. The Holy Spirit does not feel quite so safe.

2 Corinthians 3:17[B] says, "Now the Lord is the Spirit, and where the Spirit of the Lord is, there is freedom." Freedom can be a scary thing. Consider a parent with a teenager. The older they get, the more they crave freedom, and the more freedom they need in order to learn and grow. But for a parent, allowing freedom is scary. There's a good chance that teenager could make some bad choices with their freedom. The church can sometimes be like an overprotective parent. It may try to limit the freedom of its members to prevent uncomfortable situations or to try to keep out any chance of sin or failure.

The Spirit can also seem unsafe because of what Jesus said to Nicodemus when He was explaining what it means to be born again. Remember, John 3:8[C] says, "The wind blows where it wishes and you hear the sound of it, but do not know where it comes from and where it is going; so is everyone who is born of the Spirit."

There is a sense here of unpredictability. The Spirit may call you to step out in a way or time that is outside of your comfort zone and plan. The Spirit may show up in a way that you feel is undignified.

God cares about you and, in my experience, He is gentle and kind. But He's got a better plan, if you will go with it. So, in that sense, He doesn't care much for your plans, purposes, or maintaining your walls and personal dignity.

Now, Paul assures us in 1 Corinthians 14:40[A], "But everything should be done in a fitting and orderly way." He also tells us in 1 Thessalonians 5:19[D], "Do not quench the Spirit." The Spirit moves where the Spirit wills, not where we desire. The Spirit will show up in miraculous ways if we don't quench the Spirit out of our discomfort, embarrassment, unbelief, or contempt.

A couple months ago, I was looking at reviews for a book written by a prominent church leader. One of the critical reviews said, with great concern, that the book focused almost solely on the Holy Spirit and barely mentioned Jesus at all. This might seem problematic to you, but the book was mostly about the work of the Holy Spirit; therefore, it should be mostly talking about the Holy Spirit. Yet this person had a problem with that. Maybe he had a similar background to me and was taught that the Holy Spirit was important, but that Jesus should always be the focus and anything else is suspect.

The way I discovered that I truly did place Jesus over the Holy Spirit was when God showed me John 16:7ᶜ: "But I tell you the truth, it is to your *advantage* that I go away; for if I do not go away, the Helper will not come to you; but if I go, I will send Him to you." I know I must have read it before, but the truth of it had never registered.

That Greek word translated here as *advantage* is *sympherei*, which has a connotation of bringing profit and gain and advancement. It is for their profit, gain, advancement, advantage—it is better for them that Jesus goes so that He can send the Helper.

Somehow, I always felt like I would be better off if Jesus was here in physical form with me. But as I read that passage, I realized Jesus was with them and yet told them they would be better off if He left so they could have the Holy Spirit. What?! You guys, this shouldn't be a surprise, but it was to me and it was to those men with Jesus.

Now, I knew Jesus needed to die so we could be saved, but He doesn't say that it is better for them that He leaves so the world can be saved. No, He says it is better for them because they need the Holy Spirit more than they need Jesus physically with them.

Now, the Holy Spirit can live in all of us at the same time, which is certainly more advantageous than one man who physically cannot meet with every person on earth. But, Jesus seems to be saying that there is a specific benefit to those men if He leaves and the Holy Spirit comes.

These were men He was already spending all His time with, teaching and leading them.

You see, Jesus, as a person, was external, just as the law is external. Jesus says in Matthew 5:17-18[B], "Do not think that I have come to abolish the Law or the Prophets; I have not come to abolish them but to fulfill them. For truly, I say to you, until heaven and earth pass away, not an iota, not a dot, will pass from the Law until all is accomplished."

Jesus fulfilled the external laws perfectly and died a physical death to save us from the consequences of the law. But, as a man, He was an external influence in the lives of His followers. He could tell them things, but they couldn't understand. They couldn't understand, in their inner man, the spiritual things He said.

Without the Holy Spirit, we can't know Jesus or the Father in any way other than external. We need the Holy Spirit for so many reasons. Now, does this mean we should place the Holy Spirit above Jesus? No. All three persons of the Trinity are of the same importance. None higher than another. It is a privilege to know them all as one.

For now, let's look specifically at the Holy Spirit. One of my goals for the past year was to get to know the person of the Holy Spirit better. Join me on the journey.

The Holy Spirit comes alongside us as helper, advocate, and comforter

John 15:26[C] says, "When the Helper comes, whom I will send to you from the Father, that is the Spirit of truth who proceeds from the Father, He will testify about Me." The word that is translated *Helper* here is the Greek word *paraklétos*, which has a connotation of a legal advocate who advises us, helps us, counsels us, intercedes on our behalf, and comforts us.

The Holy Spirit

John is the only one who uses this word for the Holy Spirit, but Paul also speaks of this characteristic of the Spirit in Romans 8:26-27[D],

> *Likewise the Spirit also helps in our weaknesses. For we do not know what we should pray for as we ought, but the Spirit Himself makes intercession for us with groanings which cannot be uttered. Now He who searches the hearts knows what the mind of the Spirit is, because He makes intercession for the saints according to the will of God.*

The Holy Spirit convicts us

John 16:8-11[B] says, "And when he comes, he will convict the world concerning sin and righteousness and judgment: concerning sin, because they do not believe in me; concerning righteousness, because I go to the Father, and you will see me no longer; concerning judgment, because the ruler of this world is judged."

When you are sitting in church listening to the pastor or reading the Scriptures and you feel convicted, that is the Holy Spirit within you, leading you to repentance. For most people, the feeling of conviction is quite uncomfortable. But God doesn't convict us to condemn or shame us. Conviction should lead us back to God and into a deeper level of relationship with Him.

The Holy Spirit intercedes for us

The Holy Spirit speaks with God on our behalf. Romans 8:26[I] says,

> *And in a similar way, the Holy Spirit takes hold of us in our human frailty to empower us in our weakness. For example, at times we don't even know how to pray, or know the best things to ask for. But*

> the Holy Spirit rises up within us to super-intercede on our behalf, pleading to God with emotional sighs too deep for words.

He helps us when our weakness and human nature would prevent us from doing what we should. When we don't know what to do or how to pray, the Spirit steps in, if we don't give up but instead give ourselves to God.

The Holy Spirit teaches and guides us in the truth

John 14:26[C] says, "But the Helper, the Holy Spirit, whom the Father will send in My name, He will teach you all things, and bring to your remembrance all that I said to you." We need the Holy Spirit to help us understand and remember the Word of God. Furthermore, in John 16:13-15[A] Jesus says,

> But when he, the Spirit of truth, comes, he will guide you into all the truth. He will not speak on his own; he will speak only what he hears, and he will tell you what is yet to come. He will glorify me because it is from me that he will receive what he will make known to you. All that belongs to the Father is mine. That is why I said the Spirit will receive from me what he will make known to you.

Those without the Spirit moving in or on their heart cannot understand, as 1 Corinthians 1:18[D] says, "For the message of the cross is foolishness to those who are perishing, but to us who are being saved it is the power of God."

The Holy Spirit is the source of spiritual fruit

Galatians 5:22-23[B] says, "But the fruit of the Spirit is love, joy, peace, patience, kindness, goodness, faithfulness, gentleness, self-control;

against such things there is no law." It is hard to produce the fruit of the Spirit in your own effort. I've tried for years as a Christian, and I've done a poor job at producing any of them. But that's the point. If we aren't rooted in the Holy Spirit, the fruit doesn't come. I'll talk more about this in a later chapter.

The Holy Spirit is the source of spiritual gifts

In 1 Corinthians 12:4,11[E] it says, "Now there are varieties of gifts, but the same Spirit...But one and the same Spirit works all these things, distributing to each one individually just as He wills." One of the things I didn't really understand before now was the gifts of the Spirit.

Gifts of the Holy Spirit were something I wondered about and struggled with a great deal before coming to a Spirit-led church. I just felt like God had overlooked me in giving me a spiritual gift. Even though I'd taken spiritual-gift tests at different churches, they didn't do a good job differentiating between natural gifts and spiritual gifts and they excluded the more supernatural gifts like the gift of tongues, prophesy, and healing.

Now, I'm experiencing some of the more supernatural gifts, and I'm able to recognize the other gifts more easily as well. God is showing me the areas He has gifted me in, and I'm finally feeling excited about the gifts of the Spirit thirty years after being born again.

There are a few different Scripture passages that discuss and list the gifts of the Spirit. I've included several of them here. Romans 12:6-8[B] says,

> *Having gifts that differ according to the grace given to us, let us use them: if prophecy, in proportion to our faith; if service, in our serving; the one who teaches, in his teaching; the one who exhorts, in his exhortation; the one who contributes, in generosity; the one who leads, with zeal; the one who does acts of mercy, with cheerfulness.*

1 Corinthians 12:7-10[D] says,

> *But the manifestation of the Spirit is given to each one for the profit of all: for to one is given the word of wisdom through the Spirit, to another the word of knowledge through the same Spirit, to another faith by the same Spirit, to another gifts of healings by the same Spirit, to another the working of miracles, to another prophecy, to another discerning of spirits, to another different kinds of tongues, to another the interpretation of tongues.*

1 Peter 4:10-11a[A] says,

> *Each of you should use whatever gift you have received to serve others, as faithful stewards of God's grace in its various forms. If anyone speaks, they should do so as one who speaks the very words of God. If anyone serves, they should do so with the strength God provides, so that in all things God may be praised through Jesus Christ.*

Not everyone is in agreement about which gifts are available to us today, but for the moment, we will set that aside and just reiterate that the Holy Spirit is the source of these gifts and they are given to individuals to bless the whole body and bring God praise.

The Holy Spirit is our source of power

In Acts 1:8[D] Jesus says, "But you shall receive power when the Holy Spirit has come upon you; and you shall be witnesses to Me in Jerusalem, and in all Judea and Samaria, and to the end of the earth."

Then in Luke 24:49[C], He says, "And behold, I am sending forth the promise of My Father upon you; but you are to stay in the city until you are clothed with power from on high." Jesus is talking about the Holy Spirit.

The Holy Spirit

At Pentecost, the believers were filled with the Holy Spirit, which filled them with the same power that raised Jesus from the dead, and that power wasn't just to help them overcome sin. Sadly, many believers aren't even walking in that power!

How many Christians feel like they are losing a battle to sin? They haven't learned that they have power over it. But more than just that, the Holy Spirit was given in order to bring life and healing and hope through miraculous power.

Acts 19:11-12[B] says, "And God was doing extraordinary miracles by the hands of Paul, so that even handkerchiefs or aprons that had touched his skin were carried away to the sick, and their diseases left them and the evil spirits came out of them." And Acts 5:14-16[D] says,

> *And believers were increasingly added to the Lord, multitudes of both men and women, so that they brought the sick out into the streets and laid them on beds and couches, that at least the shadow of Peter passing by might fall on some of them. Also a multitude gathered from the surrounding cities to Jerusalem, bringing sick people and those who were tormented by unclean spirits, and they were all healed.*

The miraculous is something not many Christians see today. Many don't even believe it is for today. We will talk more about this in a later chapter, but we are trying to live a life that requires God's supernatural power without allowing the supernatural in. I believe this is a large reason why the church is losing people today.

The Holy Spirit is our guarantee

Ephesians 1:13–14[B] says, "In him you also, when you heard the word of truth, the gospel of your salvation, and believed in him, were sealed with the promised Holy Spirit, who is the guarantee of our inheritance until we acquire possession of it, to the praise of his glory." Having the Holy Spirit is the seal that guarantees our inheritance.

I also like the way 2 Corinthians 1:21-22[A] says it, "Now it is God who makes both us and you stand firm in Christ. He anointed us, set his seal of ownership on us, and put his Spirit in our hearts as a deposit, guaranteeing what is to come." There is a lot of talk in the church about whether or not a person can lose their salvation and how you can know you are saved. I don't want to get into that ongoing debate, but here Paul tells us that the Holy Spirit is our deposit and the guarantee of our full inheritance.

The Holy Spirit is our witness of adoption

Here again is another legal term that goes along with both the advocate and the guarantee. Romans 8:15-17[D] says,

> *For you did not receive the spirit of bondage again to fear, but you received the Spirit of adoption by whom we cry out, "Abba, Father." The Spirit Himself bears witness with our spirit that we are children of God, and if children, then heirs—heirs of God and joint heirs with Christ, if indeed we suffer with Him, that we may also be glorified together.*

When we receive the Holy Spirit, we are adopted as children of God. As mentioned before, that adoption makes us not only children who have a father, but heirs as well.

There are plenty more roles the Holy Spirit plays, but these give us a starting point. More important than knowing about the Holy Spirit is actually knowing the Holy Spirit personally as a friend. Do you know the Spirit personally?

The Holy Spirit

For a long time, I thought if the Spirit lived inside of me, everything would just happen naturally. I wouldn't need to do much. It is true that our striving won't produce fruit, but God is relational in His very nature. The Trinity, by the fact of being the Trinity, exhibits this relational nature. And for the Spirit within us to change us, we need to engage in relationship.

Now, you can focus on your overall relationship with all three members of the Godhead, and that is important. Knowing Him as a loving and good Father is so important. Knowing the person of Jesus is critical to the way we live our lives and how we relate to others. But it is the Holy Spirit within us that partners with us day in and day out in all the ways we mentioned above and more. Your life will reflect your level of relationship with the Holy Spirit.

In the same way that we begin to look like the people we surround ourselves with, we will begin to look more like Jesus the closer we engage with God's Spirit within us. Jesus only did what He saw the Father doing and said what He heard the Father saying.

How can we see what the Father is doing and hear what the Father is saying? We can only see that with spiritual eyes and ears. And how do we use those? The Holy Spirit teaches and guides us. And how can we be taught and guided by the Spirit if we don't spend time together?

You can be transformed for better or worse by building relationships with other people. How much more can you be transformed by the Spirit of God within you when you spend time with the Holy Spirit? Our hearts, our words, our actions will all be changed as we begin to be filled to overflowing.

In the next chapter, we will look at the role of the Holy Spirit in the lives of Christians in the Book of Acts and how that can relate to our lives. But before we move on, take a moment to reflect on this chapter with the following questions.

1. What stood out to you as you read this chapter on the Holy Spirit?

2. Were your expectations correct going in?

3. Did God speak to you through any of the Scriptures shared in this chapter? Which ones?

4. Which member of the trinity are you tempted to elevate above the others?

5. Which member of the trinity do you feel least comfortable with? Why?

6. How can you engage in growing your relationship with the Holy Spirit?

7. In what areas do you disagree with what was said in this chapter?

8. Where have you seen victory in your life as a result of the Holy Spirit within you?

CHAPTER 9

The Acts of the Holy Spirit

But you will receive power when the Holy Spirit has come upon you, and you will be my witnesses in Jerusalem and in all Judea and Samaria, and to the end of the earth.

- Acts 1:8[B]

You should have a basic understanding of who the Holy Spirit is after the last chapter. Now we will examine what the Holy Spirit does, specifically looking at the book of Acts.

About six months after starting to attend our new church, I was talking with one of my new friends. We were both desiring to be in a women's small group, and we began to talk about possibly starting our own group and co-leading it. We weren't sure if the logistics would work out or if the church would be open to having me co-lead since I was so new to the church, but soon after our conversation, the church offered a small group leadership training class. We both ended up going to the training and, with the encouragement of the leaders, she and I started a moms' Bible study on the book of Acts.

God just has the best sense of humor. I didn't know what I was getting into, but God did. For the first time, the book of Acts started to come alive to me. We began seeing some of the same things happening with women in our small group as the church in Acts saw. Let's dive into the Scripture and I'll share some of our experiences as we go.

In Acts 1, we find the disciples in Jerusalem following Jesus' ascension into heaven. They are wondering what will happen to them and waiting for the promised Holy Spirit. On the day of Pentecost, which is the Jewish festival of Shavuot, as the Jews (including the disciples) were celebrating God giving the Law to Moses and the Israelites on Mt. Sinai, God pours out His Holy Spirit on the disciples. This moment is so powerful and pivotal, let's look at it in Acts 2:1-4[A]:

> *When the day of Pentecost came, they were all together in one place. Suddenly a sound like the blowing of a violent wind came from heaven and filled the whole house where they were sitting. They saw what seemed to be tongues of fire that separated and came to rest on each of them. All of them were filled with the Holy Spirit and began to speak in other tongues as the Spirit enabled them.*

We will set aside the discussion of speaking in tongues until the next chapter. What I really want to show you is the complete transformation of the disciples.

People have gathered around the disciples as they are speaking in different languages, and Peter boldly addresses them and shares how Jesus fulfilled different prophecies as the Messiah. He also explains that what was happening at that moment was the giving of the Holy Spirit. Acts 2:37-40[D] says,

> *Now when they heard this, they were cut to the heart, and said to Peter and the rest of the apostles, "Men and brethren, what shall we do?"*

> *Then Peter said to them, "Repent, and let every one of you be baptized in the name of Jesus Christ for the remission of sins; and you shall receive the gift of the Holy Spirit. For the promise is to you and to your children, and to all who are afar off, as many as the Lord our God will call."*

The Acts of the Holy Spirit

> *And with many other words he testified and exhorted them, saying, "Be saved from this perverse generation."*

This is the same Peter who denied Jesus three times out of fear for his own life. These are the men who were hiding behind locked doors when the risen Jesus found them. They are the same men who went back to fishing after the risen Jesus appeared to them twice. They repeatedly saw the miraculous but never expected it. Peter was now boldly proclaiming in the streets what Jesus had done. He was testifying openly and boldly, the rest of the disciples alongside him. These men had truly been transformed.

I mentioned in one of the earlier chapters that I never really connected with the disciples after they'd been filled with the Holy Spirit. I'd much preferred reading about the people in the Old Testament. Though I accepted Jesus as my Savior at a very young age, I still remember it. I know that I received the Holy Spirit then because, as I grew, I felt the conviction of the Spirit, and would hear God talking to me through Scripture, and my desire was mostly to please the Lord.

But I was so young at the time of believing that I don't remember that first period of transformation. By the time I was old enough to study the book of Acts, I could believe, but not connect with, their experiences. I wasn't sure I wanted to connect with their experiences at that point. Persecution? No, thanks.

I love Acts 4:13[A], which says, "When they saw the courage of Peter and John and realized that they were unschooled, ordinary men, they were astonished and they took note that these men had been with Jesus." The rest of the world noticed the change as well.

It's funny, I used to focus on the part in the verse that says, "these men had been with Jesus." I believed that was why they were different. And that was important—it was the reason they could testify about Him. But they did not testify boldly about Jesus until the Holy Spirit came and filled them.

I have often been afraid of what the Holy Spirit might ask me to do. I've been around other people who, in vulnerable moments, shared the same feelings. We were worried the Spirit might call us to go to some remote part of the world and live in a hut and share the gospel. Or more realistically, we were afraid the Holy Spirit would call us to go up to a stranger and tell them about Jesus, or worse, to a friend we didn't want to offend.

I'm pretty sure if I'd known a few years ago that the Holy Spirit would tell me to write a book, about my personal faith, with controversial beliefs in it, with my name on it, I might have spent a lot of time feeling panicked.

In this moment, I realize I have really been transformed. I can feel the fear trying to rise in me about publishing this book, but mostly I have a sense of peace that is beyond my understanding. I have no idea what the reach of this book will be, but I expect I will have my own share of critics.

I will tell you that God has been so gentle and kind to me on this journey. There have been moments where God has asked me to do uncomfortable things. He started out small and slowly asked more and more. But the more I step out and say yes, the more excited I am (although still nervous beforehand) to say yes again. Because the more I step out, the more God shows up and reveals Himself to me. And I just want more and more of Him.

Let's dive back into Acts. In Acts 4, Peter and John had to stand before the Jewish rules, elders and High Priest to account for healing a man. They preached boldly about Jesus and salvation. The Jewish leaders threatened them and told them to stop speaking about Jesus.

When Peter and John went back to the believers, they talked and prayed together. One of the things they prayed for was *boldness* to keep speaking the truth. They *didn't* ask for less persecution. They *didn't* ask for someone else to step in. They asked for boldness in the face of more persecution.

I love Acts 4:31ᶜ: "And when they had prayed, the place where they had gathered together was shaken, and they were all filled with the Holy Spirit and began to speak the Word of God with boldness."

Have you ever been in a prayer meeting that ended with the place being shaken? They left with the boldness that they had been praying for. Are your prayers being answered? Have you tried praying for boldness in whatever circumstance you are in?

In my moms' small group, we started praying for boldness. We came in timid and, by the end, the Lord was answering our prayers. It was certainly less intimidating praying for it together. Do you have someone you could ask to pray with you for boldness? If you don't, you can certainly do it on your own. But there is something powerful and encouraging about being a part of a group moving forward together in boldness.

We also have Jesus' promise in Matthew 18:20ᴳ, "For where two or three are gathered in My name [meeting together as My followers], I am there among them." We heard many testimonies as women stepped out of their comfort zone and reached out to strangers. We saw people encouraged and healed in our group and outside of our group.

The apostles in Acts continue to see miracle after miracle. People are healed, thousands believe and are baptized, the gospel spreads. As their numbers grow, they start running into problems such as widows being overlooked, deception from their own, and increased persecution. But we see again and again that they rejoice in the midst of trials.

I would say that I didn't see or hear about many people rejoicing in trials in my previous church experiences. It could be that it was happening, and I just didn't know about it. In the church I'm at now, we hear testimonies all the time of people worshiping and praising God in hospital rooms, in prayer closets, and we see them dancing or kneeling in worship in the front of the church in the midst of overwhelming trials and tragic situations.

So far we've only been in the first few chapters of Acts and already we see the power of the Holy Spirit on full display. And yet, it is only the beginning.

In Acts 9 we see another person who is powerfully transformed by the Holy Spirit—the apostle Paul. We talked about his transformation at the beginning of this book, but it was amazing! From persecuting believers, to boldly proclaiming the gospel throughout the region, to enduring many hardships for the sake of the gospel—including, eventually, the loss of his life—Paul shows us that the Holy Spirit's transformative abilities know no bounds.

Then we see the Holy Spirit move both Peter and Paul to minister to the Gentiles, and we see the Spirit poured out on believing Gentiles, even before they are baptized with water, in Acts 10:44-48[E],

> *Even as Peter was saying these things, the Holy Spirit fell upon all who were listening to the message. The Jewish believers who came with Peter were amazed that the gift of the Holy Spirit had been poured out on the Gentiles, too. For they heard them speaking in other tongues and praising God. Then Peter asked, "Can anyone object to their being baptized, now that they have received the Holy Spirit just as we did?" So he gave orders for them to be baptized in the name of Jesus Christ.*

This was a huge adjustment for the Church at that time, which was mostly made up of Jewish believers. But this was always Jesus' purpose, to open salvation to the Gentiles as well. Praise God for choosing us to be grafted in!

Not only did the Holy Spirit lead them to the major change of welcoming Gentiles, but He led them through the transitional period of adjusting to all these new believers who had completely different backgrounds. The Holy Spirit led them to move forward together in unity.

As we met together for our study of Acts, we kept finding ways the Holy Spirit was working in our group. I realized that the Holy Spirit was not at all staying within the bounds of my expectations. In one of the early weeks of our Bible study, one of the women shared that God will tell her to go to a certain store or stop at a certain place when she is out running errands. She experiences it somewhat regularly and she obeys. She told us about a specific example that happened just that week where God told her to go to a place and she had a God encounter with a woman who needed to be blessed in a specific way by God.

Her story is another example of how God is still working in the ways He did in the book of Acts. In Acts 8:26-31[A], The Holy Spirit tells Philip to go a certain direction,

> *Now an angel of the Lord said to Philip, "Go south to the road—the desert road—that goes down from Jerusalem to Gaza." So he started out, and on his way he met an Ethiopian eunuch, an important official in charge of all the treasury of the Kandake (which means "queen of the Ethiopians"). This man had gone to Jerusalem to worship, and on his way home was sitting in his chariot reading the Book of Isaiah the prophet. The Spirit told Philip, "Go to that chariot and stay near it."*
>
> *Then Philip ran up to the chariot and heard the man reading Isaiah the prophet. "Do you understand what you are reading?" Philip asked.*
>
> *"How can I," he said, "unless someone explains it to me?" So he invited Philip to come up and sit with him.*

Philip then explains that the passage the man is reading is a prophecy that Jesus fulfilled, and he shares the good news of Jesus with him. They pass a body of water and the Ethiopian asks to be baptized. As a result of Philip following the Holy Spirit, this man is saved and baptized! And as my friend's experience shows, God is still leading people in this way today.

I've noticed that I passionately ask God for guidance in areas of my life, but then I tend to get frustrated when He doesn't answer right away. I would like to consider for a moment that perhaps we don't wait in the right way. When frustrated, we tend to step away. We wait while distracting ourselves with other things, by decompressing and taking a break from life. The things we distract ourselves with may not be sinful, but they are a step away from God because we feel like He is being silent.

Let's look at Acts 13:2[B] and see what the early church was doing when the Holy Spirit gave them guidance. "While they were worshiping the Lord and fasting, the Holy Spirit said, 'Set apart for me Barnabas and Saul for the work to which I have called them.'" God is not temperamental. He wants us to see what He is doing and join Him. He wants us to listen to His instructions and follow them.

If you are waiting for an answer, don't get discouraged. Worship God and praise Him while you wait. If you feel called to fast, then fast. God hasn't spoken to me much about fasting from food. I'm in a season of life with small children where I feel the need to be mentally clear, and I need food for that.

But I do at times feel God calling me to fast from other things for a certain period. Sometimes it is from a certain form of social media, or from a certain way of relaxing, like reading fiction. I'm fasting several things while writing this book. Fasting from these methods of distraction for a season helps me to face the areas of lack and discomfort in my life that I'm avoiding and refocus on what the Lord is doing in those areas. Whichever way you feel called to refocus on the Lord, do it in those times of waiting.

There are so many more works of the Holy Spirit in the book of Acts and throughout the rest of the New Testament, but we will end the chapter with the Spirit compelling Paul to go to specific places while also warning him of what he will face. Acts 20:22-24[A] says,

> *And now, compelled by the Spirit, I am going to Jerusalem, not knowing what will happen to me there. I only know that in every city the Holy Spirit warns me that prison and hardships are facing me. However, I consider my life worth nothing to me; my only aim is to finish the race and complete the task the Lord Jesus has given me—the task of testifying to the good news of God's grace.*

Have you ever felt compelled by the Holy Spirit to do something that you know will be uncomfortable? It is hard to obey in those moments. I still find it hard most of the time, but in certain areas, I find it almost as if God has made a way for me to look past the discomfort and see clearly that good will come from it. And when I see what the good might be for His kingdom, then I can more confidently step into uncomfortable areas.

My discomfort is no match for the trials Paul faced, and the good results my little steps may bring cannot match the victories Paul achieved, but I've been called to be obedient with what I have. Whether you have been given little or much, you will be called to account for what you've done with what you were given (Matthew 25).

So now it's your turn.

1. Which part of this chapter most stood out to you?

2. Have you ever felt like the book of Acts came alive to you? What was that experience like?

3. Has God ever led you to talk to someone you didn't know? What happened?

4. What results have you seen stepping out in faith in ways you feel uncomfortable?

5. Have you ever prayed for boldness? What was the result?

6. What do you do when God seems silent when you ask for direction?

7. What is your experience with fasting?

8. Do you feel prompted to take any specific actions after reading this chapter? If so, what actions? Are you going to follow through?

CHAPTER 10

God's Miraculous Power

For this reason I remind you to fan into flame the gift of God, which is in you through the laying on of my hands, for God gave us a spirit not of fear but of power and love and self-control.

- 2 Timothy 1:6-7[B]

Part of me has always been suspicious about anything too emotional or feelings-related. And I was even more suspicious about claims of miraculous signs. For some reason, I associated miraculous signs with televangelists, who could be claiming anything, without accountability.

But, even before we found our new church and began to see the miraculous, God had begun showing me verse after verse about God's power that was available to me. I really didn't know what to do with those verses. The church I knew seemed to have power similar to the rest of the world—mostly based on self-effort. Christians tried hard, but were constantly busy, tired, and overwhelmed. The church mentality was that the world was getting worse and worse and it would continue to go that way until the Lord's return. The worse it got, the faster He'd come back.

In chapter eight, I mentioned that receiving power is part of receiving the Holy Spirit. When you receive the Holy Spirit, you receive His power (Acts 1:8). I hadn't seen that. If God still performed miracles today, why wasn't I seeing them? Why were so many churches convinced that those gifts were not for today? I don't know for sure, but I think Matthew 13:57-58[D] gives a good starting point, "So they were offended at Him. But Jesus said to them, 'A prophet is not without honor except in his own country and in his own house.' Now He did not do many mighty works there because of their unbelief."

Unbelief seems to limit what God will do, just as faith seems to draw God to us. It seems that these churches' lack of faith that God will show up in certain ways may actually be the reason He doesn't show up in that way—a self-fulfilling prophecy. If you don't pray for and step out in faith to see miracles, then you won't see them.

Now, could God still do miracles there? Nothing is impossible with God. But He seems to have set up this system, a natural law of sorts, that faith is the conduit for the miraculous. Not just faith that Jesus died to save us, but a belief that He wants to show up in our lives in miraculous ways. Hebrews 11:6[C] says (emphasis is mine), "And without faith it is impossible to please Him, for he who comes to God must believe that He is and that He is a *rewarder of those who seek Him.*"

It is also clear that the promise of power can draw out people with the wrong motives and can possibly corrupt those with the right motives. Acts talks about a sorcerer trying to buy the power to lay hands on people and give them the Holy Spirit (Acts 8:9-25). Many churches want to avoid power because they see it as corrupt.

Many modern-day churches seem to be afraid of power. But Paul says in his letter to the Corinthian church in 1 Corinthians 4:18[A] (emphasis is mine), "Some of you have become arrogant, as if I were not coming to you. But I will come to you very soon, if the Lord is willing, and then I will find out not only how these arrogant people are talking, but what power they have. *For the kingdom of God is not a matter of talk but of power.*" Paul seems to be saying that all talk and no power shows you are not of the Kingdom of God.

Another possible reason for so many churches not seeing miraculous power has to do with the body of Christ. We are called to be the body of Christ. Jesus has returned to the right hand of the Father, but He has commissioned us to continue His mission here on earth with His Holy Spirit's help. Somewhere along the way, from those first years until now, things got pretty divided in the body. As I consider all believers across the world, I see a body that is fractured, broken, and filled with enmity between its parts.

People tend to find and gather with people who look, think, and act like them. They gather with others who have similar passions and priorities. All the right hands are gathering in one place, rejecting the left hands, and the neck, and the head. The head is rejecting the hands and the feet.

Each part thinks its role is most important, when really, if we could see the big picture, we'd do a whole lot better supporting and encouraging each part. Those who believe in the miraculous gather together. Those who dislike power because it might be abused gather together. Those who might be okay with power but aren't quite ready to step all the way in—they gather together.

The body has lost its sense of purpose. If we are to be the body of Christ, shouldn't we look like Jesus did when He was here on earth? What did Christ's physical body do? He healed all the sick who came, He taught those who would listen, He discipled those who followed Him, He took time to pray and talk with the Father, He freed people who were troubled by the demonic, He called those He healed to turn from sin, He saw what the Father was doing and partnered with Him, He stood up for the downtrodden, He ate with sinners and outsiders, He called out the religious leaders for their failures. He proclaimed that the Kingdom of Heaven was at hand.

He didn't *just* feed the poor. He didn't *just* heal the sick. He didn't *just* teach the people. In a way, it does make sense for people with similar passions to work together to make a bigger impact. One person helping the poor makes a small difference. Five hundred people helping the poor make a bigger impact. But if a church only has people focused on the poor, who will teach? Who will disciple? Who will heal?

Even if we want to mostly surround ourselves with those to whom we are similar, perhaps we should also start recognizing the value of churches that have other parts of the body, celebrate the ways they look like Jesus, and perhaps even partner with them from time to time. For instance, I'd like to celebrate the Baptist church. I've only occasionally attended Baptist churches, but my life has been blessed in many ways by Baptist churches I don't even attend! The ones I'm familiar with truly know how to do community outreach.

I could tell you the benefits of so many of the denominations, but this chapter has other purposes. I hope you will take up the exercise and consider another denomination outside your own and see how it looks like Jesus.

In my desire to know and grow more, I've turned to watching and listening to some other Spirit-led teachers online. In that process, I have encountered ideas that are not biblical. I've also encountered ones that are biblical but clearly don't stem from a heart of love, but from a seemingly self-righteous heart. I've also found some ideas that seem solid and stand the test of Scripture.

The Spirit-led churches don't necessarily have all the right answers. Its leaders aren't any less likely to be flawed than any other denomination or group of Christians. The leaders can and do still fail just like leaders in other denominations. But its leaders can also be walking closely with the Lord, just like leaders in any other denomination.

In my own journey, God has revealed Himself to me in such an amazing way through coming into a Spirit-led church that really tries hard to get it right, takes risks to step into the power of the Holy Spirit, and isn't afraid to admit when it fails. It has been a safe place to learn about the gifts of the Spirit.

I'm still learning, but I've had some pretty significant moments related to the gifts of the Spirit that I'd like to share with you. There are some vulnerable moments in this chapter and no condemnation on any side. I hope you'll journey with me and stick it out, even if you aren't sure about these gifts of the Spirit.

Speaking in tongues

I usually try to see all sides of an issue honestly before deciding where I stand. I tend to research things into the ground. Although I prided myself in thorough examination, I had never really looked at all sides of Spirit-led gifts.

The only time I truly remember even thinking about any of them was back in college when I was talking to a guy who was part of a church where everyone spoke in tongues. Their position was that if you were saved, you could speak in tongues. And I told him I was saved, but I didn't speak in tongues. He said he'd pray for me and I should receive it. So, he did, and nothing happened. He couldn't understand why. As a result of that experience and from realizing that many Spirit-led churches believe that not speaking in tongues is a sign you aren't saved, I've avoided the Spirit-led churches and denominations.

Despite that, for a very long time, I've had a deep, hidden desire to be more filled with the Spirit. In honest moments, I knew something was still missing, and I longed for more. One Sunday at our previous church, the pastor taught about the Holy Spirit. I don't remember a word of the sermon, but my heart was burning within me. At the end, the elders came to the front to pray for people who wanted more of the Holy Spirit.

Even though I'd been saved for years, I desperately wanted a greater measure of the Holy Spirit if there was more. I don't like standing out, so part of me was hesitant to go forward, but I found that I could not stay in my seat.

The elder, a wonderful man we knew, prayed over me when I told him through tears how I felt and what I wanted. I had hoped there would be some sign afterwards that the prayer had been answered, but I saw nothing. I'm not saying there was no answer, but if there was, it was unseen. That was years ago.

When we ended up at our new church, one of the pastors would get up after worship and say things that sounded like speaking in tongues, but initially I wasn't really sure if it was tongues or just another language she already knew. The tongues never lasted long and seemed to just be part of the transition out of worship into the next thing.

At times people in the congregation would speak in tongues when the worship moved into a less structured time. But there was very little talk and focus on the gift of tongues. I was far more confused and interested in other gifts that were being used, like prophecy, to spend much time thinking about tongues.

Though my interest in tongues was relatively mild at this point, my husband and I had found a podcast by a couple in which they rationally explained different topics from a Spirit-led viewpoint, and I noticed one morning that they had one on speaking in tongues. They rationally explained the gift of tongues, their personal experiences with it, and then prayed for people to receive it.

As I was reflecting on it later during my quiet time, I was listening for the Lord. For me it started with hearing one syllable, speaking it, then hearing another and speaking it. And then the floodgates opened. I found I was suddenly speaking and praying in tongues.

God's Miraculous Power

I know I already had the Holy Spirit in me before that, but now I was walking in a gift that somehow I'd always had but never knew how to access. I can't explain why that was the moment. If you have never spoken in tongues, it doesn't mean you aren't saved. I will say that I do believe it is available to all believers who desire it, but that many have never found a way to access it.

Since that day, I've learned more about how the gift of tongues works for me. I do not have much control over it. That first day I prayed for about an hour, hardly being able to stop. In the days and weeks that followed, it died down to a trickle. There were days where I could only repeat one phrase over and over—I don't know what I was saying. There were many days at the beginning when I wondered where all the words had gone and if I had imagined the whole thing.

Over time, as I kept praying, more and different words started returning. One night I woke up in the middle of the night and felt moved to pray in tongues for a long while. Pretty much what I seem to be able to control is whether to open my mouth and say the words and when to close my mouth and stop them. And not always even that.

I don't pray in tongues every day, but I find it such a release when my heart is moved either in anguish or joy to pray words that seem to express far more powerfully what I can't express on my own. And when I'm praying for others and I don't know how to pray, I love using it then. I am no better for having the gift. I am not more loved or more worthy. But I understand more clearly God's desire to give us good gifts. I feel His joy when I use a gift He's given me.

In the back of this book is a list of resources for those interested. The information about the podcast is there for those who would like to hear it. I pray if it is your heart's desire to be able to speak in tongues, that God will reveal to you how to access this gift. He's a good Father. He loves to see His children using His gifts.

Prophecy

While I had heard about tongues before coming to a Spirit-led church, I had never really heard about people today walking in the gift of prophecy. The first time someone got up and prophesied at our new church, I was extremely uncomfortable. I really wasn't sure that God was behind it. I didn't like the awkwardness of the times when no one seemed to receive the word.

At that point, I even questioned if we'd really heard God correctly about this being the right church. (This was many months before I received the gift of tongues.) But God reaffirmed to me we were at the right place and told me just to hold off on deciding anything. So, I'm going to ask you to settle in for just a bit and hold off deciding anything. You can always close the book in a few minutes.

Anyway, we kept going, studying the Word, growing, and accepting what was good and setting aside things we weren't sure about. The church kept having prophetic nights, but the dates were never ones we could make. Finally, a prophetic night came up that we could attend, and we decided to go see what it was about. I was still somewhat skeptical, but I reasoned that going to get a prophetic word should help me decide if it was real or not.

I'd never received a prophetic word before. I didn't know what to expect at all. When it was my turn with one of the prophetic groups, I tried to go with an open mind, hoping they would say something profound or call out a hidden desire I had for the future so I would be convinced. But what they said felt like safe, generalized, encouraging words that didn't really feel profound or confirming.

While I didn't feel convinced by my experience that the prophetic was real, I did feel better about the way they executed it. They were straightforward about the fact that they prophesy in part. They also brought up

1 Thessalonians 5:20-21[D] which says, "Do not despise prophecies. Test all things; hold fast what is good."

We were encouraged to test it, and examine it, and only hold on to what was true. So, I left still feeling doubtful about prophetic gifts, but encouraged that it wasn't completely outside of scriptural guidelines.

I still wasn't very comfortable with the prophetic by the time my friend and I started attending the training sessions in preparation to co-lead a Bible study together. The first night of the training, we came to the end and the pastor said we were going to play a prophetic activation game before leaving. I was trying to think of a subtle way to sneak out, so I didn't have to participate.

But I didn't, and the game ended up not being weird or scary at all. We simply shared, with a randomly assigned person, the first thing that came to mind after the pastor gave us a prompt.

We did a brief game each of the four weeks of training, and while I didn't dread them after the first week, I was still skeptical that what we were sharing was from the Lord and actually prophetic. I did see that people were encouraged by the words, and some seemed to be accurate, but they tended to be a bit generic.

Skip forward a couple weeks, and my friend and I were planning out our first week of Bible study. She was going to lead the first lesson, and she asked me to lead a prophetic activation game before the lesson. Here I am, not even sure what I believe about prophetic, leading the prophetic part of a Bible study.

I was honest with the women that first week about not being qualified or even sure. But while skeptical, I was willing to continue testing it since I'd overcome the initial discomfort in those four weeks. As we practiced these prophetic activations each week, I slowly began to realize that some of the words we were getting (completely not knowing who the word was for) were really connecting. And the time was always encouraging and filled with the love of Jesus.

As I learned to listen for God and discern His voice in my own life, as well as in those prophetic games, I began to really appreciate them. You see, sometimes when I tried to hear God about situations in my own life, it was hard to distinguish if I'd heard right or not. But in a prophetic activation game, I had someone giving me immediate feedback about how accurate I was.

Less than a year later, I felt God telling me to step out in faith in the area of prophetic ministry. So, I signed up for the prophetic team, which gave me the opportunity to start hearing God for other people on a larger scale—to help them start their own conversations with God. I was thankful for a place that was safe to learn, question, grow, step back, disagree, and experience.

The prophetic has no place in my old theology. There is no room to fit it in. There is only room for it when I realize the prophetic only comes when I step out in faith and risk to share something I heard for someone else. They then get to talk to God about it and decide whether it was from the Lord or not. Either way, the word I share will hopefully start their own conversation with God.

Paul spends time teaching about prophecy. It's listed in several Bible passages that talk about the gifts of the Spirit. He even tells us to eagerly desire it in 1 Corinthians 14: 1-3[D].

> *Pursue love, and desire spiritual gifts, but especially that you may prophesy. For he who speaks in a tongue does not speak to men but to God, for no one understands him; however, in the spirit he speaks mysteries. But he who prophesies speaks edification and exhortation and comfort to men.*

Our prophetic team always abides by the verses from 1 Corinthians 13:1-2[B],

> *If I speak in the tongues of men and of angels, but have not love, I am a noisy gong or a clanging cymbal. And if I have prophetic powers, and understand all mysteries and all knowledge, and if I have all faith, so as to remove mountains, but have not love, I am nothing.*

Every word given by our team needs to be filtered with love. If it is not coming from a place of love, it doesn't qualify because love is more important. I believe that prophetic words given this way are edifying to the body, and I've come to see that God does speak through us to other people.

I know I've heard things for people who are strangers that touch them deeply. Often the words that touch people the most are the ones that I almost don't say because, based on my first impression of them, I didn't think the word could possibly be right for them.

Looking back now, more than a year after receiving those first prophetic words given to me, I see that many of them were far more specific than I realized. As God has started speaking His call over my life, I see that some of those words are clearly and directly in line with where God is taking me.

I like where our church stands on the issue of prophecy—we know in part, we prophesy in part, we do it out of love, and the person receiving gets to test and decide if they receive it. I feel nervous every time I get ready to give a word. I wonder if God is going to speak, but the reward is worth overcoming the fear. People leave so encouraged.

I really love hearing God speak and helping other people start up their own conversation with Him. In the next chapter we'll talk more about hearing God's voice, but I would say that learning to prophesy jump-started and encouraged me as I learned to recognize God's voice for myself in my own life.

Healing

Whew! Whether you made it through the prophetic section or skipped ahead, I'm glad you're here. The idea of miraculous healing was both easier and harder for me to come to terms with. This was one of the things I most wanted to believe but was also most offended by. I was offended because I've prayed hard for people who were never healed.

At my previous church, one of the pastors, who seemed to have God's heart for people, said something like: "When I pray for someone, I pray expecting that God will heal that person. That's what the Bible says we need to do to see answered prayers. God doesn't always heal the person, but I see more healings when I pray expecting that God wants to heal them, so I always pray believing and expecting healing."

I was comfortable with that idea. Praying with full faith brings better results than praying but not expecting healing. I saw that it was in line with James 1:6-8[A], which says, "But when you ask, you must believe and not doubt, because the one who doubts is like a wave of the sea, blown and tossed by the wind. That person should not expect to receive anything from the Lord. Such a person is double-minded and unstable in all they do." The problem was, it could be hard to be convinced that God was going to heal when I prayed, since I knew they might not actually be healed.

But now I was at a church that said whether healing happens or not, in every single incidence, God wants or wanted to heal. Why the healing doesn't always happen is unknown, but the heart of God is to heal, not to kill, steal, destroy, give someone cancer to make them stronger, or have someone die so someone else can come to faith. That pushed hard against some pretty good experiential theology I had.

God's Miraculous Power

I felt like the idea that God always wanted to heal could really do more harm than good when talking to people who'd had experiences in life that showed them otherwise. How much hurt could it bring to say to someone who had a loved one die that God had wanted to heal them here on earth, but they still weren't healed? I wrestled with the idea for a long time.

After some consideration, I decided I was willing to test believing God always wanted to heal and see what happened. Our pastors hadn't grown up believing in healing either, but said that they saw a whole lot more healing now than they ever did when they didn't believe God wanted to heal one hundred percent of the time. I naively assumed that I could always go back.

Less than a month after making my decision to test the belief that God wanted to heal one hundred percent of the time, I got a message that my cousin's two-year-old son, Max, was in the hospital following a serious accident. Though our extended family lives a good distance away, I would consider us relatively close knit for an extended family. She had been a bridesmaid in my wedding. My heart ached for her and her family, but I immediately began to pray and believe for them.

Almost everyone in my extended family is a believer. My dad and his brothers grew up on the mission field in the Middle East. They were all praying for a miracle. I prayed, believing one hundred percent that God wanted to heal and would heal Max. I asked others at our church to pray who'd been believing and practicing this longer than I had. I fully believed he would be healed. I was so very sure God was going to show himself faithful and solidify my belief in healing. But healing didn't come. Max died.

I'm sure I don't need to say it, but that wrecked me. My heart was broken, and I was devastated for his family. I was devastated for my extended family. Even though my grief isn't even close to the grief of his parents and immediate family, it broke something deep within me in a way beyond what it probably would have if I hadn't been so confident in God's desire to heal.

Beyond just the grief of losing Max and grief for his family, I also didn't know how to trust God anymore or what to believe about healing. My son had just turned two at the time, and I didn't know how to trust God with the life of my own children.

I didn't have my old theology to fall back on. My old theology said that it was God's will for that little boy to die. But I had been learning that God didn't kill, steal, or destroy. So where was God? Why hadn't He heard? We had believed one hundred percent that God wanted to heal Max. What went wrong?

A few months later, I decided to check out an inner healing session our church was offering. I was not thinking about Max's death when I signed up. I had rebuilt just enough theology to get on with life while still grieving every time I saw a photo or thought of my cousin or snuggled my own two-year-old close. I didn't think I really needed inner healing. I just went to see what it was about.

I was not thinking about or planning to share about Max, but when it was my turn to talk, instead of sharing what I planned to say, the whole story about Max just poured out. I was a complete, sobbing mess. I was encouraged to lay bare all my hurt and questions before God and be open to what He wanted to say about it. I left lighter for having shared and grieved, but still with no closure or answers.

About a week later, I had my first real, heart-to-heart talk with God, where I know He spoke back to me in an actual conversation. He talked to me about Max. He did not answer my "why" question, but He answered a lot of other questions. I've since learned that He doesn't often respond to "why." Maybe it's too big for us, maybe it's too accusatory, but I've learned in order to talk with Him, "why" is often the wrong question.

In those moments when I was talking to God about Max, God mourned with me over his death. He mourned with me even though Max is now happily in heaven with Him. And even though He has used Max's death to work many good and wonderful things, God does not say that his death was good.

Shortly after that experience, I watched a message by a prominent man in the healing movement about when healing doesn't happen, and something he said stuck with me. He's seen multitudes of people healed, but he's also seen people and kids die, even after he's prayed for healing for them. He said that instead of letting doubt creep in during those times, he presses in and grows his faith even more, so that the next time he prays healing for a dying child the result might be different.

Hearing those specific words wrecked me again. I was ready to shrink back from this new faith because I felt disillusioned, hurt, and like a failure. I wanted to say this kind of faith doesn't work. I wanted to protect myself and others from unmet expectations. But if I gave in to those feelings, how could I ever hope to be ready for the next person who needed my prayers. If there was even the smallest possibility that I could change the outcome of a similar circumstance in the future by holding on to my new faith, it is worth the cost.

As I considered this, I ran across Hebrews 10:38-39[C] which says, "But my righteous one shall live by faith; And if he shrinks back, My soul has no pleasure in him. But we are not of those who shrink back to destruction, but of those who have faith to the preserving of the soul." I will choose not to shrink back.

Since that time, I've seen with my own eyes many people at church miraculously healed of different ailments. I've also seen plenty not get healed. My old theology doesn't have room for miraculous healing. I'm not planning to make a new theology. I'm just going to simply say, I believe God does heal supernaturally and instantaneously today.

I also clearly see that the people who believe God wants to heal one hundred percent of the time are the ones who see people healed. I don't yet know anyone who experiences healings one hundred percent of the time. I have seen a couple of healings myself when praying, but certainly not every time.

When I was first trying to decide how I felt about the belief that God wants to heal all the time, I read someone's thoughts about a leading figure in the healing movement who has an adult son who is still partially deaf to this day. This stood out to me because I have a son who is deaf in one ear.

The criticism leveled at the movement and the leading figure because his son has not yet been healed (as well as other health issues they pointed out surrounding that leader) initially made me take a big step back and agree with the critic. Who was this guy to say that God wanted to heal every single time when he hadn't experienced it fully in his own family? The critic didn't deny that there had been other miraculous healings, just that the leader couldn't heal himself or his own son.

Recently I've been thinking more logically about this leader. He started mostly unknown. When he began to lead his church into this belief about healing, many left the church. So, he certainly didn't start out doing it for fame or money. He stepped out in risk because he believed God wanted to show up. How much more of a mental battle must it have been when he didn't see healing in his own child? And yet he didn't give up and many people are miraculously healed regularly as a result of his ministry.

Our church is continuing to see more and more healings. Is every single person healed? No, at least not instantaneously. Does that mean it was not God's will to heal them all? I would submit the answer is also no.

God recently gave me this analogy, which has helped me with my struggle in thinking about God's will. (This is not to condemn anyone and I'm only including it because it is a powerful analogy.)

God's Miraculous Power

Is it God's will for married couples to get divorced? I would submit that the answer is no, based on many Bible verses including Malachi 2:16 and Mark 10:2-12. Do married couples still get divorced? All the time. Does that then mean that it is God's will since it happens all the time? No. Does that mean that God is not sovereign because His will was not upheld? No. Does that mean God can't or won't still bring good out of divorce situations? No. He does bring good out of bad situations. Romans 8:28[A] says, "And we know that in all things God works for the good of those who love him, who have been called according to his purpose."

Before we can even begin to believe that it might be God's will to heal all the time, we must believe that God isn't the one who gives sickness, injury, and death. In Matthew 12:25-28[D], Jesus responds to the Pharisees who believe that Jesus is casting out demons by the power of the devil. He says,

> *But Jesus knew their thoughts, and said to them: "Every kingdom divided against itself is brought to desolation, and every city or house divided against itself will not stand. If Satan casts out Satan, he is divided against himself. How then will his kingdom stand? And if I cast out demons by Beelzebub, by whom do your sons cast them out? Therefore they shall be your judges. But if I cast out demons by the Spirit of God, surely the kingdom of God has come upon you."*

God's kingdom is not divided. He doesn't give sickness just to take it away. Jesus only healed people. He didn't give any of them sickness. James 3:10[B] says, "From the same mouth come blessing and cursing. My brothers, these things ought not to be so." God doesn't both bless and curse us. I'd submit that He's not even just sitting there and allowing us to be harmed.

If you'd like to get technical, you could say that He is allowing the world to continue in sin and decay, which is allowing sickness and death, as He waits, wanting as many people as possible to come to salvation before

Jesus' return. Psalm 115:16ᴱ says, "The heavens belong to the Lord, but he has given the earth to all humanity."

As a result of our dominion, which led to a fallen world, sin, sickness, and death entered. They affect all of us in our natural state of being. God is looking for people to partner with Him in bringing heaven to earth, and thereby healing to people who need it. Jesus taught us to pray in Matthew 6:10ᴬ, "Your kingdom come, your will be done, on earth as it is in heaven." There is no sickness or pain in heaven.

James 5:14-15ᶜ says,

> *Is anyone among you sick? Then he must call for the elders of the church and they are to pray over him, anointing him with oil in the name of the Lord; and the prayer offered in faith will restore the one who is sick, and the Lord will raise him up, and if he has committed sins, they will be forgiven him.*

There is no asterisk here. It says, if the church prays over them in faith, the sick will be restored, and their sins will be forgiven. Now if you didn't get healed, we *don't* say that your lack of faith or your secret sin kept you from healing. No, the faith this Scripture is talking about is on the side of the church, the elders, and those praying for the sick.

We also don't say that the person must have hidden sins that are getting in the way. That Scripture says when you pray for healing, "the Lord will raise him up, and if he has committed sins, they will be forgiven." The prayer brings both healing and forgiveness of sins. Forgiveness of sins isn't even first in this verse, it is secondary.

Jesus healed everyone who came to Him. Acts 10:38ᶜ says, "You know of Jesus of Nazareth, how God anointed Him with the Holy Spirit and with power, and how He went about doing good and healing *all* who were oppressed by the devil, for God was with Him."

God's Miraculous Power

The more our church and pastors and congregation have believed and agreed that God wants to heal one hundred percent of the time, the more often we step out and pray for people, and therefore the more people we do see experience instantaneous healings. At previous churches, we almost never saw people healed and, if they were, it was usually a result of medical treatment being successful (though this can still be God answering prayer), not instantaneous healing.

Even so, there is this gap between what is believed and what is experienced. There are still people who are not healed. I would love to know why. But I don't. I joined the healing team to grow my faith, to believe more, to see more healings, and to be part of something I feel God is bringing through our church.

I have decided I'd rather believe that God wants to heal one hundred percent of the time, even if I pray and still see nothing, than to believe God only wants to heal occasionally and miss partnering with God to bring healing to people who are sick and hurting and dying.

It isn't easy to believe. It is much more painful to believe and not see healing than it is to believe it wasn't God's will to heal and then to comfort ourselves with that assurance instead. But, I'd rather feel the pain and press in so I can help someone else have healing in the future. I'd rather pray believing hundreds of times for healing, even if I feel the pain of no immediate result ninety-five percent of the time, than to never pray for healing and never feel the pain.

In Max's honor, I will believe that God is good, and that God wants to heal, even when I don't see it. I will not shrink back but will press in. What the enemy intended for evil, God already has and will continue to use to bring about good.

Now, I am not in any way saying that people should not go to doctors for treatment. We have access to amazing medical technology and talented men and women who serve in the field of medicine. Let's allow them to be witnesses to the miraculous healing we expect God to do. And when there is a gap between what we believe and what we see, we are so thankful that God can and does answer prayers through doctors and nurses and hospitals.

Also, no one should ever deny that they are sick or hurt when they clearly are—how can you be healed if you don't say you need healing? And absolutely no one should ever agree they are healed when they are not. It's far better to honestly say that healing didn't happen and try again than to fake it.

As I sit here editing this chapter, I have one of the worst colds I've ever had. And less than a week before I got this cold, my whole family had just finally gotten healthy after having been sick with the flu for over a week. We prayed and believed over the kids, we prayed and believed over ourselves, we had many people at church praying over us.

I am thankful to God for the medical professionals in my life since there was a gap between what I believe and the reality I was living in. In health or in sickness, I will praise God for His goodness and thank Him for the amazing people He placed in our lives who are praying for and believing with us for health.

I may not have created a theology about healing, but I have decided that I will have faith and believe that God's will is to heal one hundred percent of the time, even when I don't see it. I don't know if my faith is right or wrong. I've come to terms with the fact that being right isn't a fruit of the Spirit. I'd rather err on the side of more faith in God than less. I look more like Jesus now, believing God wants to heal people from sickness, than I did before.

If you are where I was more than two years ago on my journey, I'll be surprised if you made it through this chapter without putting up at least some walls. It was a major transition for me mentally. Even still, I'm continuing to grow in it and walk in it. I will leave you with some Scriptures which played a huge part in showing me my previous theology wasn't based on Scripture.

Matthew 10:7-8[D] says, "And as you go, preach, saying, 'The kingdom of heaven is at hand.' Heal the sick, cleanse the lepers, raise the dead, cast out demons. Freely you have received, freely give."

John 14:12-14[B] says, "Truly, truly, I say to you, whoever believes in me will also do the works that I do; and greater works than these will he do, because I am going to the Father. Whatever you ask in my name, this I will do, that the Father may be glorified in the Son. If you ask me anything in my name, I will do it."

Galatians 3:3-5[C] says, "Are you so foolish? Having begun by the Spirit, are you now being perfected by the flesh? Did you suffer so many things in vain—if indeed it was in vain? So then, does He who provides you with the Spirit and works miracles among you, do it by the works of the Law, or by hearing with faith?"

Mark 16:17-18[A] says, "And these signs will accompany those who believe: In my name they will drive out demons; they will speak in new tongues; they will pick up snakes with their hands; and when they drink deadly poison, it will not hurt them at all; they will place their hands on sick people, and they will get well."

I know many people who dismiss the verses from Mark because of the part about snakes and poison. I've heard of extreme churches that attempt snake handling or other outrageous acts to show their faith in God.

I would ask, who does it benefit when venomous snakes are handled, or poison is consumed without harm? But on the other hand, who does it benefit when the enemy is driven out and the sick are healed?

God's promise of protection should be an encouragement in difficult circumstances rather than a show for personal gain, but God's desire to heal people through us shouldn't be thrown out because of sensationalists.

Now it is your turn for further reflection.

1. What is your initial response to this chapter?

2. Have you been turned off to the miraculous gifts of the Spirit in the past? Do you believe they are for today or do you believe they have ceased?

3. If the gifts of the spirit aren't all available, why would we be told to eagerly desire certain ones?

4. Have you ever spoken in tongues or been around someone speaking in tongues? How does it make you feel?

5. Is it more correct to base our theology on our personal experience or on what the Word of God says?

6. How often do you pray for healing? When you do, do you pray believing that God wants to heal?

7. Have you struggled with healings that didn't come? How did you come to terms with it?

8. What are your thoughts about the response to healings that don't happen?

9. Which of the three gifts of the Spirit that I mentioned are you most comfortable with? Which one are you least comfortable with?

10. Where will you go from here?

CHAPTER 11

Hearing God's Voice

*My sheep hear my voice, and I know them,
and they follow me.*

- John 10:27[B]

The last chapter was weighty, but I see this one as the light shining in! Learning to hear God's voice is the best part of my journey over the past two years. It is still an ongoing process, but one that is a joy to press into. The same podcast I mentioned before, that I think helped me access my ability to speak in tongues, also has some good episodes about learning to hear God's voice. Hearing God is the piece of the puzzle that has helped me grow so much in the areas I have. Without it, I would not be writing a book right now.

I think what amazed me most was that God doesn't just want to speak to us, but that He is speaking to us in so many different ways even today. I knew about most of them from Bible stories, but I did not know many of them were still available today. Life looks so different when you start being aware of all the ways God is speaking and start truly hearing His voice regularly.

The following list is not comprehensive, but here are some ways people heard God in the Bible and some ways I've encountered now that will hopefully help you expand your expectations and help you in your own journey to hear God better.

God speaks through the Bible

I knew God spoke through the Bible. That was the main way I used to hear Him and is still a powerful way I hear Him today. The Spirit will nudge me or show me a verse, and it will just click, and I'll realize God is speaking to me. 2 Timothy 3:16-17[A] says, "All Scripture is God-breathed and is useful for teaching, rebuking, correcting and training in righteousness, so that the servant of God may be thoroughly equipped for every good work."

The Bible is also where we see and hear what Jesus did and said. Romans 10:17[B] says, "So faith comes from hearing, and hearing through the Word of Christ." Even now that I hear God in other ways, I regularly ask God where to read from, so I often find Him speaking powerfully from His Word to my heart and mind.

God speaks through Christian books

The same thing that would happen when reading the Bible would also happen with Bible study books or other Christian books, where the Holy Spirit would highlight something to me. The Bible should always be our main source for truth, but sometimes hearing a Christian author reframe something or highlight something in a book or Bible study will resonate in our hearts, and we know God is teaching us or correcting us or encouraging us through what we read.

Now, all Christian authors are imperfect. Just as no church has all the right answers, Christian authors will also get things wrong. But just because one part of a book or Bible study is in contradiction to what you believe doesn't mean God can't speak to you through another part of the book. I've found numerous times where I disagreed with what the author said in one place but still heard God speaking to me in a different part of the book.

Always read with the Holy Spirit to guide you and guard you, but be careful not to be so superior in your beliefs that you throw out the good because of the bad. 1 Thessalonians 5:21[C] says, "But examine everything carefully; hold fast to that which is good." We should never be so comfortable that we stop examining what we read or so critical that we cannot read any book other than scripture.

God speaks through other Christians

I also knew that God spoke through pastors, ministers, reverends, etc. Occasionally on Sunday mornings in church, I would feel like there was some piece of the sermon or message that God was specifically saying just to me. Of course, God is also speaking on Sundays when I don't feel like the message is targeted to me, but there are moments where it just really feels direct.

God had also spoken to me through friends and women in my Bible study. Not in a prophetic way, but just in sharing their story or insight, I would feel God speaking to me where I was in that moment through their comments or their own experiences.

God speaks through music

I often hear God through music, both in the past and still today, mostly by the lyrics saying exactly what my heart needed to hear, but sometimes just in the instrumental parts. Especially now that I've learned how to seek out God's presence, I find that just a few notes will draw me in, and I'll hear Him speaking to my heart in a language beyond words.

I was part of an event at my church recently, and those of us serving had arrived early. The person leading worship was setting up and rehearsing in the main sanctuary while several of us were talking in the foyer. The first couple of chords were so anointed that we just stopped talking and couldn't help but go on in to listen and worship. God was speaking and didn't care that it was a rehearsal.

God speaks through creation

God speaks to me through creation, especially looking at a vast ocean, or a sunset, or the night sky. In those moments, I'm drawn to praising Him. Psalm 19:1-4[A] says,

> *The heavens declare the glory of God;*
>   *the skies proclaim the work of his hands.*
> *Day after day they pour forth speech;*
>   *night after night they reveal knowledge.*
> *They have no speech, they use no words;*
>   *no sound is heard from them.*
> *Yet their voice goes out into all the earth,*
>   *their words to the ends of the world.*

Creation speaks in a language that crosses time and culture and reaches deep to touch any who would stop to look.

God speaks audibly

I know Christian friends and leaders who have had an experience where God spoke to them audibly, but I have not yet heard Him this way. Most of those who have heard this way said it was a one-time event. We know God spoke audibly to people in the Bible even long before Jesus came. 1 Kings 19:12-13[C] says,

> *After the earthquake a fire, but the Lord was not in the fire; and after the fire a sound of a gentle blowing. When Elijah heard it,*

he wrapped his face in his mantle and went out and stood in the entrance of the cave. And behold, a voice came to him and said, "What are you doing here, Elijah?"

Here God speaks to Elijah in an audible gentle whisper. In 1 Samuel 3, we see that Samuel also hears God audibly when God first calls him.

Another example is when Jesus was baptized. Luke 3:22[D] says, "And the Holy Spirit descended in bodily form like a dove upon Him, and a voice came from heaven which said, 'You are My beloved Son; in You I am well pleased.'" There are more examples, but these show that God does speak audibly to people.

God speaks through dreams

I had also heard one or two people say that God had spoken to them through a dream, but I didn't really think that was something I could or would experience. My husband has always liked to talk about his dreams, but more in the "I had a weird dream" sense, not in the "God gave me this dream" sense.

I was never really into talking about dreams at all, as I viewed them mostly as random creations of a person's brain, and I found listening to other people talk about their dreams rather boring.

Once we learned that dreams are one of the ways that God still speaks, I encouraged my husband to write his down. After a while, I decided it wasn't a bad idea to write mine down as well. It wasn't until one night where I had two very strong and slightly disturbing dreams that I really believed God might speak to me in dreams.

You see, the two dreams were completely different in every way except in the theme. Both seemed strongly like a warning—and even though they were disturbing, I was far less upset and frightened in the dream than I should have been. Upon waking, I immediately remembered stories about Joseph in the Bible that involved two different dreams with the same meaning. You can see those examples in Genesis chapters 37, 40, and 41. I realized that my dreams were like that and had spiritual meaning to guide me if I'd listen.

Since then I've had a few more dreams that are very obviously from the Lord, as well as many that are probably just normal dreams or much more subtle in their meaning. My husband had one very profound dream which was so biblical that I even found a verse that it related to directly in the Bible—a verse he had no knowledge of.

The thing about dreams, though, is that they are often more like the parables of Jesus. You must begin to understand the symbolic way God likes to talk through pictures and symbols and themes. As I began to examine dreams, God began showing me throughout Scripture the way He speaks in parables and stories and analogies. Go to God for the interpretation—just like Joseph and Daniel did.

God speaks through images and visions

One way that God speaks, which was completely foreign to me before, is in visions. I didn't remember getting pictures in my head in the past, but once we came to our current church, I would occasionally see images during worship. Just brief pictures through which I felt God was speaking to me. It is possible that God was trying to speak to me in this way before, but I never paid attention.

Now, there are different kinds of visions, and those pictures I would get are sometimes referred to as inner visions. They are often, but not always, the way God speaks to me when I receive a prophetic word for another person.

Another kind of vision is called an open vision. This kind is more like a projection around you while you are still aware of your current surroundings. I have experienced this type of vision, but not often. In my understanding, these are less common than the first type, but more common than the third.

The third type of vision is often called a trance, and it is what John experienced when he wrote the book of Revelation and what Peter saw in Acts 10. In a trance you are completely in the Spirit realm and not aware of your surroundings on earth. It almost always has auditory and visual aspects. I have not experienced this, and I don't know anyone who has, but I do believe God still speaks in this way.

For those skeptical that visions and dreams are for today as I was, God led me repeatedly to Acts 2:17[A] which says,

> *In the last days, God says,*
>   *I will pour out my Spirit on all people.*
> *Your sons and daughters will prophesy,*
>   *your young men will see visions,*
>   *your old men will dream dreams.*

When you haven't experienced it yourself or known anyone close who has, it can be hard to believe. I thought it was only available in rare instances and for special people. But what if God is already speaking to you in your dreams, or in brief images that come into your mind, but you have been dismissing them because you didn't realize God might be using them to communicate something to you?

The easiest way to test it is to start writing them down. Then keep writing them down, even if you don't think they mean anything. For both my husband and me, it took a while of writing down our dreams before we began to have ones that we knew were clearly from the Lord. I know other people who have them right away.

God speaks in our mind

Possibly my favorite way, but also one of the hardest to dial in, is God speaking directly to my mind. I can't believe how long I was a Christian without knowing God was speaking to me. We talked about how I learned to recognize and separate my own thoughts from His thoughts and from the enemy's thoughts. Sometimes I'm completely certain it is God speaking, and sometimes I'm still uncertain, but I write what I hear, and I test it against Scripture, and I check with other believers.

The reason I like this way God speaks so much is that I can have a two-way conversation with Him. I can sit down and have a quiet time and hear Him speak. I can ask questions and sometimes He answers. But the best way to hear Him talking is just to ask Him what He wants to say. I'm just so overwhelmed by God's kindness and love in the way He speaks. I know the more time I spend with Him, the more I will be able to discern His voice. John 10:4b[c] says, "the sheep follow him because they know his voice." Do you know His voice?

God speaks through prophecy

I know I shared that I was originally suspicious of prophetic words. But even when I was skeptical, I made sure to write down each one I've been given in the past year and a half so that I can test them. Plenty are somewhat vague and more encouraging than anything else, but some have really resonated as God speaks to me very specifically about what He is calling me to do.

In fact, I had received a seemingly random prophetic word less than two weeks before God told me to write this book. When God then called me to write the book and confirmed the subject, I realized that the word I had been given, which was not specifically about writing a book, actually confirmed the topic and revealed how God wanted to use my story.

1 John 4:1[C] says, "Beloved, do not believe every spirit, but test the spirits to see whether they are from God, because many false prophets have gone out into the world." We need to be aware that there are false teachers and false prophets, but that shouldn't scare us away from what is good. Again, 1 Thessalonians 5:20-21[D] tells us, "Do not despise prophecies. Test all things; hold fast what is good."

In my life, learning to record and test prophetic words has led to increased intimacy with God. I'm not sure that every word I was given was directly from God, but if it isn't, I can let it go and just hold fast to what brought good fruit.

Also, as I mentioned before, hearing prophetic words for others has helped me recognize God's voice more clearly.

God speaks through physical sensations

This final way God speaks is one that seems so bizarre to me. I cannot find this in Scripture, so take it as you will, but I have seen it in practice. In the simplest form, I have experienced it as heat or tingling.

My son was sick with a stomach bug one night near the beginning of our journey in healing. He had woken up in the middle of the night and we did our best to make him comfortable and help him. I'd finally gotten back in bed, but I noticed that my hands were getting hotter and hotter, unnaturally so.

I remembered that other people at church had talked about heat sometimes preceding a healing. Part of me felt like I must be imagining it. But they got hotter and hotter, so I got back up and went and laid hands on my son and commanded the sickness to leave. After praying, the heat left my hands and he went back to sleep and had no further stomach bug symptoms.

I have also seen this when our pastor will give a word of knowledge about something God is about to heal because he is experiencing it in his own body, and it isn't his own pain or sensation. I once experienced someone else's physical sensations myself when I was serving on the healing team. It seemed so natural in the moment, but looking at it from a logical standpoint, it is just so hard to wrap my head around.

There are plenty more unique ways God spoke in the Bible—through a burning bush (Exodus 3), through a donkey (Numbers 22), through dry or wet fleece (Judges 6), through the Urim and Thummim (Exodus 28:30), through casting lots (Joshua 7), and through angels (Genesis 18). We now have the Holy Spirit, so we should be able to hear what the Lord says without rolling dice, but don't limit God's ability to speak through only the ways you are comfortable hearing Him.

I told someone the other day that I feel as if I'm addicted to hearing God's voice. It's why I signed up to be on the prophetic team, to hear God's voice more. In this season, it seems easier for me to hear what God is saying to someone else, especially before I even see their face or know who they are. That way I'm less likely to be influenced by situations and prior knowledge and put my own twist on what I feel God is saying.

Learning to recognize God's voice has been a process. The more I write down both my dreams and what I think God is speaking into my mind, the more I hear, and the more I'm aware whether I heard accurately or not in what I wrote.

I have a theory that it is easier to recognize God's voice when you first believe, if you know how to listen. I didn't have any expectation of God speaking to me as I was growing up, so I didn't listen as much for His voice. As a result, I never became sensitive to it. But there's still hope to learn to hear Him better, as I am doing now. If you want to hear God better, I suggest you start writing down what you think you hear. Then be sure to test it.

Sometimes God speaks to us and asks us to do hard or uncomfortable things. Certainly, we need to test those against Scripture and with other people we trust, but most of the time the reason they're hard is because they require us to take a risk. The times when I'm tempted to resist God, I think about what I might miss out on if I don't follow His leading.

If I believe He is a good Father, I know that anything He is leading me to do (which will not be in opposition to what He says in Scripture) is for my good—and possibly the good of many other people as well. Obviously, you should always test what you hear against Scripture and check with several other people you trust who also recognize God's voice before taking any major questionable steps. God's Word is always our benchmark and guide.

The other thing to be cautious of as you hear God more and more is not to neglect talking to Him. I was so excited to finally hear God more clearly, I almost stopped speaking to Him except to hear Him in return. I'm learning it is a balance.

We are all called to pray continually (1 Thessalonians 5:16) and to pray with thanksgiving about everything (Philippians 4:6). Prayer is powerful and important and should not be neglected, which means whether we hear God talking to us in the moment or not, we should always be interceding on our side. God loves to speak, but He also loves to hear us and answer our prayers.

So, it's your turn once again. Take time to consider the following questions.

1. Which of these ways have you experienced God speaking to you?

2. Which one is the way He most often speaks to you?

3. Which one is your favorite way He speaks?

4. Which one would you like to experience that you haven't yet?

5. Which one are you most doubtful of?

6. Do you keep track of what God says to you? How?

7. Do you test what you hear God saying to you? How?

8. Have you ever loved hearing God so much that you forgot to talk to Him and intercede for others on your end?

9. What is the most powerful prayer you have seen answered?

CHAPTER 12

Our Testimony

Always be prepared to give an answer to everyone who asks you to give the reason for the hope that you have. But do this with gentleness and respect, keeping a clear conscience, so that those who speak maliciously against your good behavior in Christ may be ashamed of their slander.

- 1 Peter 3:15b-16[A]

We are all on a journey. You've heard some of mine. I hope someday, somehow, I might hear yours. In the resources section at the back of the book, I'll provide a website where you can share with me if you'd like. The testimony of what God has done in our lives is meant to be shared. We are to tell and declare what God has done for us.

Psalm 66:16[B] says, "Come and hear, all you who fear God, and I will tell what he has done for my soul." And in Luke 8:39a[I] it says, "Return to your home and your family, and tell them all the wonderful things God has done for you."

Whether you ever share your story with me or not, I hope you will find people around you to share it with. Your testimony could be a moment of breakthrough for them. Your testimony isn't just about when you received Jesus and the trials you've walked through. It's about what God is doing in your life now. It's about what He is teaching you and how He's preparing you and what you feel called to in the future. And remember, your testimony (and mine) are not finished yet. God still has so much to do in and through us. He has so much more He wants to teach us and reveal to us when we are ready.

Let go of who you think you are supposed to be and ask God who He created you to be. What dreams has God given you for your life? How does He want to use you for His glory? How can you move mountains for His kingdom alongside Him? Whatever it is, Hebrews 12:1^C says, "Therefore, since we have so great a cloud of witnesses surrounding us, let us also lay aside every encumbrance and the sin which so easily entangles us, and let us run with endurance the race that is set before us."

It won't always look easy, but we have the Holy Spirit in us, and we have access to the power that raised Christ from the dead. 1 John 5:4^B says, "For everyone who has been born of God overcomes the world. And this is the victory that has overcome the world—our faith." Keep in mind the importance of faith and remember the victory is already won!

When I first started getting prophetic words, people kept speaking the word "hope" over me. I didn't believe them. I didn't see myself as a hopeful person. I was and am a realist. I didn't really have much hope in God. I was a bit too nervous about (what I believed to be) His unpredictable nature to be overly hopeful. But the more I have pursued God's presence, and the more I have heard Him speak, the more hope I have, and the more I see myself in the word "hope." I pray that in some way I have given you a bit of hope from my testimony.

I'll leave you with a final challenge and a blessing from Scripture.

What if we are missing out on God's plan because we are more concerned with defending our perfect theology than with knowing God and sharing Him with the world? What if we miss out because we are more concerned with our outward persona than with our inward heart? Are we merely whitewashed tombs?

What if the things we fear are the things we need to run toward? What if our fear is the enemy's way of keeping us from what God has for us? What if our greatest fear is an indicator of where God wants to give us our biggest victory?

What steps can you put in place today to move forward in knowing God? What risks can you take to open the door for Jesus to show up? What area is God calling you to step out in? What passion has He placed within you? Will you join me in stepping out?

"May the God of hope fill you with all joy and peace as you trust in him, so that you may overflow with hope by the power of the Holy Spirit." - Romans 15:13[A]

Acknowledgements

Lord God—my shepherd, my banner, lover of my soul—I am so grateful that you revealed yourself to me in a new way, invited me deeper into relationship, showed me my identity in you, and gave me hope and a destiny. Thank you for calling me to author this book and giving me the grace and ability to finish it.

Brian—my amazing husband—I am beyond grateful for all the times you watched the kids while I wrote and edited this book. Your feedback, when you were able to read my drafts, was very much appreciated as well, especially when I began the editing process. Thank you for seeing my worth and what I have to offer and encouraging me to step out. You always look for ways of making space for me to follow my passions and calling.

Papa—thank you for making sure we always went to church as a family. I'm appreciative, now, that you sneakily helped me memorize Scripture by "requiring" me to help you memorize Scripture in the car on the way to school. I'm glad it sunk in despite my annoyance as a non-morning person. Thank you for always being willing to use your talents to help me and thereby teaching me to use my talents to help others. You also showed me how important it is to take a stand for what I believe, even if it might not be popular.

Mama—there isn't enough room to thank you for everything, so I'll just choose a few. Thank you for letting me cry and helping me process predestination when I was wrestling hard with theology during college. I greatly value your gentleness and kindness and friendship. Thank you for somehow knowing how to perfectly balance encouraging my independence and always being available when I need you. I can only hope my children will one day look at me the way I look at you. I see now that you always knew I had the ability to fly.

Peter and Masha Oswalt—this book is a result of all that I have learned at your feet. Thank you for showing me the heart of God, for encouraging my questions, and answering them in ways that left me seeking more of God. Thank you for leaving room for me to be taught by the Lord and for helping me see that risk of failure is the key to success.

Rhonda Fleming—thank you for seeing my vision for this book. Your expert advice and editing made my rambling thoughts shine. Thank you for your genuine excitement about what God will do with it. You are a pleasure to work with!

Meagan Davenport and Rebekah McCullough—when I think of you both, I feel such love and tenderness that cannot be conveyed in words. Though life has taken us on our own paths, the bond we formed as children still remains. Meagan, thank you for the time you took to read my final draft and give me your expert opinion on everything from content to fonts. Your feedback was invaluable, and I loved connecting with you throughout the process. Rebekah, thank you for your ongoing vulnerability and for graciously allowing me to share the hardest moments of your life and the ways it affected me. I appreciate how genuine you are in all that you do, and that you were genuinely excited for me and this book.

Rian Davis and Nataliya Limonchenko—thank you for encouraging me as I wrote this book and believing in me even when I was about ready to give up. Thank you for praying with me, growing with me, fighting my battles with me, and for sharing your battles with me. Rian, thank you for making the time in a busy season to read and give me feedback on the first draft of this book.. Your contagious excitement about what God will do with it keeps me going. Nataliya, thank you for being a gentle and quiet strength in my life and a safe place to process as I walked through much of the content of this book.

Acknowledgements

Anne Say—thank you for your excellent advice on the business side of writing and challenging me to create a vision beyond the book. I'm so thankful that God told me to call you. I appreciate you always making time to chat with me when I have questions and sharing wisdom and encouragement as I've walked through this process.

Coty and Katie Sloan—thank you for coming to the rescue and helping me with the book cover. Your work propelled the design to a truly professional level. I greatly appreciate your humble and generous attitude toward the project, but even more so your friendship and encouragement in this process.

My other Arise:Life Bible study ladies—thank you for praying for me and with me as I wrote this, and for encouraging me along the way. Carole Palmer, thank you for cheering me on as I wrote, for walking with me through hard things, and for the amazing chicken soup! Jill Hawes, thank you for being someone who truly makes me feel heard and for seeing something of value in me. Thank you for letting me share my successes and challenges along the way. Katie Hester, thank you for the words you've spoken over me and for sharing your story with me—you have helped me better understand how God wants to use me. Stephanie Mitchell, thank you for showing me your unwavering faith and sharing testimonies to raise our faith. Thank you for giving me a safe place to explore healing and prophecy.

My Arise:Life Church family—thank you for being my spiritual family. Thank you for worshiping wholeheartedly so that the Spirit of God shows up in power. Thank you for welcoming us and walking with us. Thank you for being a safe place to grow, to fail, to mourn, to celebrate, and to walk in the Spirit. Without you, there would be no book.

To all the godly people who have poured into me throughout every season of my life—as I begin to think of you, I realize just how many of you there are—thank you. You each helped me in a step of my journey. You propelled me to a place of being ready for more. You supported me where I was at the time. I am incredibly grateful for you all.

Resources

Here are some resources referred to throughout the book as well as other resources you may find useful.

- Speaking in tongues podcast episode 184 by Alyn and AJ Jones
  (if you know nothing about Alyn and AJ, you may want to skip past the update about their life)

  *Go to **alynandaj.com/podcast** and search for **Episode 184***

- Hearing God's voice podcast episode 204 by Alyn and AJ Jones
  (if you know nothing about Alyn and AJ, you may want to skip past the update about their life)

  *Go to **alynandaj.com/podcast** and search for **Episode 204***

- Blog posts by Emily Fieg:

  *Go to **EmilyFieg.com***

Find a list of more resources and share your feedback and testimony at PhariseeSetFree.com

About the Author

Emily Fieg is a daughter of the King. She has a bachelor's degree in English from Presbyterian College. She has attended church regularly all her life and has been a Christian for over 30 years. Unfortunately, quite a few of those years were spent as a Pharisee.

Emily lives in Acworth, Georgia, with her husband and children.

To learn more about Emily, you can go to EmilyFieg.com

Made in the USA
San Bernardino, CA
01 May 2020